Stepping Stones

More Daily Meditations for Men

FROM THE BEST-SELLING AUTHOR OF *TOUCHSTONES*

Hazelden
Publishing

Hazelden Publishing
Center City, Minnesota 55012
hazelden.org/bookstore

ISBN: 978-1-61649-828-3

Library of Congress Cataloging-in-Publication
data is on file with the Library of Congress.

Editor's notes

Stepping Stones was formerly titled *Wisdom to Know*. In the process of being
reissued in 2019, this book has undergone minor editing updates and been re-
typeset in the Whitman font family.

To the greatest degree possible, the accuracy of quotations and sources has
been verified.

23 22 21 20   2 3 4 5 6

INTERIOR DESIGN: TERRI KINNE
TYPESETTING: PERCOLATOR GRAPHIC DESIGN
REISSUE DEVELOPMENT EDITING: MINDY KESKINEN

Serenity Prayer

God, grant me the serenity
to accept the things I cannot change,
courage to change the things I can,
and wisdom to know the difference.

Introduction

That first small group of men in Ohio who had been lost in the wilderness of alcoholism searched and struggled to find a way out. With no path to follow, they forged a trail that became a way into sober adulthood. We now follow their path like a trail of stepping stones into spiritual awakening.

In this book of meditations, I was inspired by the founders of the Twelve Step program who used the metaphor of "steps" to mark the path they found to successful recovery from alcoholism. And the path also shows the way to recovery from addictions of every type as well as codependency. As I now page through this retitled edition of the book formerly called *Wisdom to Know*, I recognize three recurring themes: *recovery as a path, becoming grown-up in our masculinity*, and *awakening our spirituality*.

We are *walking a path*, and our main tasks are to stay on the trail and to make progress. It is sometimes an adventure, sometimes challenging, and often a joy. We may get off the track at times and find ourselves at a dead end, or stuck. Our motto is "Keep coming back. Keep returning to the way." Our goal is not to arrive at perfection; it's not to climb a ladder to reach closer and closer to perfection, but simply to keep coming back to the path.

Masculinity is much more than being competitive, tough, and aggressive. Those may be a boy's idea of what a grown-up man is really like. Tough and aggressive are fine traits, but when they are over-developed as the main qualities of a man, his personality becomes brittle, more easily broken, and lacking in wisdom, honesty, or love and respect for himself and others.

On this path, our *spirituality wakes up*. It's an adventure in which we experience an aliveness and awe for the life that surrounds us. We still encounter fear and anger, but now we find new and more effective ways to deal with them. Peace of mind replaces negative feelings.

Many of my friends and family members took an interest in the creation of this book. They mined their own treasuries of quotations and offered them as inspirations. Some sent me favorite quotes that they kept on their bathroom mirrors or under refrigerator magnets. Others brought their collection of best-loved quotes they had gathered over the years. To all of these friends and loved ones, I say thank you.

—M.A.F.

JANUARY

Hope smiles on the threshold of the year to come,
whispering that it will be happier.
— *Alfred, Lord Tennyson*

At the start of this new year, we look back at what has been, and we look forward to the future. Our path has been filled with healing and hope. Rewards have come to us each day. Now, looking toward the year ahead, we can't know much of what will happen, but we can recommit ourselves to our healing and sober path. We can have renewed comfort and optimism that we will not be alone and that we will be able to handle whatever comes our way.

The start of a new year is a good time to make lists of the things we fear, the things we hope for, and the things we are grateful for. These lists serve as a kind of snapshot inventory of our attitude toward the world and our relationship with our Higher Power. They point a direction for us today and for the year ahead. We can put these lists in a safe place until next year, when we will bring them out as a reminder of where we were and a measure of how far we've come.

Today, I once again turn my life and will
over to the care of God.

Nothing is predestined: the obstacles of your past can become gateways that lead to new beginnings.

— *Ralph Blum*

At this doorway to a new year, we look ahead to new beginnings. In some ways, this is like any other day in the cycle of our lives. Some things we know for sure, and other things are yet to be revealed. We can know that again on this day we will stay sober and true to our path of healing and recovery. Still, we look to the year ahead with a sense of adventure. This year will be a continuing flow of experiences, and on this path, we deal with each experience with the calm certainty that we are not alone. We know that we cannot control what happens to us, but we can stay true to ourselves. "Keep coming back" is a well-known motto for our life in recovery. We are not perfect, and we don't expect perfection of ourselves. What we expect is to keep returning to our path. Like any driver or any pilot who continuously reorients his craft as he travels along his route, we look forward to this year, knowing that we will keep returning to the true course we have chosen. It will be an adventure, and we will take whatever happens and use it for our growth.

Living one day at a time, my pledge is to keep coming back to this path of renewal.

A marriage without conflicts is almost as
inconceivable as a nation without crises.
— André Maurois

Conflict is not bad; it is necessary. In any good, intimate partnership, the two people reveal themselves to each other. As they reveal themselves, their differences sometimes are interesting and enjoyable and sometimes create conflict. A good conflict is open and honest and without ego. When one person reveals his or her thoughts, the other person listens and hears them as a genuine expression that must be taken into account. The simple act of listening is usually most important; agreement isn't always necessary. Most of the time, a person just wants to be heard. Agreement is required when there is only one path that can be chosen. Then, the wisdom of two loving and honest people can lead to a mutual agreement that often turns out to be better than either individual path.

The true, unique nature of any intimate partnership only takes shape through genuine conflict and resolution. Crises faced and resolved become the foundation for continuing and deepening mutual understanding and intimacy.

Today, I will not avoid conflict but will face it
with honesty and an open heart.

Be patient with everyone, but above all
with yourself.
— *Saint Francis de Sales*

The path of healing and recovery sets challenging standards. We are asked to "turn our will and our lives over," to be "searching and fearless" in our moral inventory, and to make amends to all those we have harmed. Many of us have lifelong habits of over-criticizing ourselves and condemning ourselves for who we are. When we face challenging standards, we can't meet them perfectly. This is a program of progress, not perfection.

If we are not seeking to attain perfection, then we need to deepen our understanding of what we *are* seeking. The answer is in the slogan "Keep coming back." It's a slogan usually applied to the idea of continuing to return to meetings, even if we don't see our way clearly at first. But it also applies to meeting standards. We don't seek perfection; we seek to keep coming back to the Steps of recovery because it is a given that we will keep falling off them. It is only when we stop returning to the Steps that we get seriously off track.

Today, I will be patient with my progress
on this healing journey.

No winter lasts forever; no spring skips its turn.
— *Hal Borland*

In the midst of winter, the short days and the long nights may seem to last forever. But we know that the turn of the cycle is inevitable. Every winter is followed by spring. When we feel depressed and discouraged, we may not feel optimistic about anything. We may not see the path from here to a place where life feels brighter and warmer. That is when we must remind ourselves that all things eventually change. We do find life beyond our current problems. We do regain our energy and our joy in life.

All pain is finite. It has its beginning and its end. Our path may require us to learn to endure and live with some pain. Some Native Americans' training for youth included fasting and solitary journeys that strengthened them and showed them how to deal with shortage and difficulty. Life must contain dark times, and when we learn that we can carry on until we find light, we have something permanent to fall back on. While we may feel pessimistic, we can remind ourselves that it is only a feature of our current mood, not a permanent state.

Today, I live in the knowledge
that spring is eternal.

*Music washes away from the soul
the dust of everyday life.*
— *Berthold Auerbach*

We need ways to express what we have experienced. Expression gives form to our experience and allows us to move on. Music taps into our deeper self and evokes feelings that we may not otherwise have access to. It conveys what is otherwise inexpressible and opens a channel to the spiritual world. Some of us love to make music, and all of us can listen to it.

When asked to describe how we make contact with our Higher Power, some men have said that it's mainly through music. The great religious traditions of the world all use music: hymns, bells, chanting, drums. But we don't necessarily need religious music to make conscious contact with our Higher Power. A good song on the radio can do it.

*Today, I will let music speak for me of things
I cannot say in plain words.*

If you want others to be happy, practice compassion. If you want to be happy, practice compassion.

— *Dalai Lama*

The word *compassion* means literally *to suffer with* someone. We normally use the word more broadly to mean empathize, or feel, with a person. Moving out of the prison of our own self-centeredness, we grow in the ability to see the world through the eyes of others. We grow wiser and more effective in our own lives because we aren't limited to one outlook. We learn to forgive ourselves and suddenly we are much freer with our forgiveness of others.

There is a generosity of spirit in compassion, and the most generous attitude comes when we can act compassionately with someone we don't especially like. Even though we may not choose a particular guy to be our best friend, we can accept and honor the hard times he has had, and we can put ourselves in his place to see what his challenges have been. Nothing is more admirable than a strong man acting generously and compassionately toward another human being.

Today, I will strive to be generous with compassion and to see the world as someone else sees it.

Lead us from the unreal to the real world.
— Hindu invocation

In pursuit of pleasures and escapes during our active addiction, we created a bubble of unreality around ourselves. Stepping into the bubble was exciting; it carried us off into gambling, or erotic and romantic pursuits, or online escapes, or shopping, or alcohol and other drugs, or the codependent thrill of trying to scoop other people out of their troubles. We used a whole system of half-truths and self-deceit to allow the bubble to exist. It led us to become more self-centered and more grandiose as we tried to force the unreal world to exist in reality.

Now, as we live in freedom from our addictive and codependent behaviors, we continue to peel back the layers of unreality. We no longer fight with reality as it is, or try to shape and mold it to fit our desires. We see more clearly by living more honestly. One of the benefits of our new life is that we feel clearheaded. Life seems simpler now, and we feel a peace of mind that we could not have even imagined in the past.

*May I continue to see and accept
reality as it is given.*

*God's admiration for us is infinitely greater
than anything we can conjure up for Him.*
— *Saint Francis of Assisi*

Those of us who look back on a trail of guilty feelings and
shame may find it hard to fathom God's admiration for
us. This whole idea, which comes from a Christian saint
who lived eight hundred years ago, turns upside down
our ideas of a God who is watching us and counting
all the things we have done wrong. But we have been
created to have a place here. And we have a right to take
our place among all of God's beloved creatures.

No matter how imperfect we are, no matter what we
feel guilty about, no matter how low our self-esteem,
we are living in the grace of a God who loves us and
holds us close, even at our lowest point. We sometimes
feel alienated from God. We have difficulty making
conscious contact. Even then, we can still know that
God carries us through these hard times.

*Today, I will walk in the light of God's admiration
and accept it to the best of my ability.*

*The fearless are merely fearless. People who act
in spite of their fear are truly brave.*
— James A. LaFond-Lewis

Fear plays a role in our lives in different ways. Many of us
have been so conditioned to deny fear that we don't even
know we are afraid and are, in fact, reacting to it. We may
look back on a major life choice and realize we chose one
job over another because of fear. Some of us can see in
the rearview mirror that our controlling ways rise out of
fear, not desire for power. The fact is that until we allow
ourselves to know our fears, we will react impulsively to
them and cannot respond bravely to them.

Our fears don't give us a license to control those
around us. Our fears don't make our addictive escapes
any less harmful. On this path, we seek to know our
fears, to call them by name so we can be smart in dealing
with them. Sometimes we may use our fear as wise guidance to avoid danger, and other times we may choose to
bravely step into the circle of our fear and face it down
because we do not want to be irrationally ruled by it.

*Today, I will open my eyes to see my fears and then
choose wiser, braver responses to them.*

When I hear somebody sigh, "Life is hard," I am
always tempted to ask, "Compared to what?"
— *Sydney J. Harris*

There is no question—life is hard at times. None of us
escapes trials and challenges. And some of us truly seem
to have more of them than others. So what are we to do
with that realization? We cannot control most of what
happens to us. We can only control how we respond to
it. No two paths are the same. Self-pity is the response
of someone who hasn't yet learned to deal with adult
life. Feeling sorry for ourselves is like having a hole
in a bucket that allows our spirit and our strength to
drain away.

Instead of reacting with self-pity, we remind ourselves
that all things change and the difficulty we face today will
also change. What is harder for us today will be easier
tomorrow. We will have times of peace and satisfaction.
Best of all, when we play a bad hand well, we have peace
of mind, our inner strength grows, and we have something more in our bank of knowledge.

Today, I am grateful for life itself.

*When we try to pick out anything by itself,
we find it hitched to everything else in the
Universe.*

— *John Muir*

Some days our lives seem to be in chaos. We may feel
flooded with too much: too much work, too much pain,
too much to learn, or too many problems to handle. On
days like this, we can begin to see past the chaos and feel
hopeful about dealing with the future because we can
turn to our Higher Power.

All things are part of a larger whole in the universe,
and all things are connected. We are never completely
alone. There is comfort and security in knowing that we
can rely on our Higher Power. We only have to do a small
part today. The universe will continue to work its way
toward a natural solution to today's problems.

*Today, I will concentrate on simply doing
one small part of what needs to be done.*

Go confidently in the direction of your dreams!
Live the life you've imagined.
— Henry David Thoreau

To have a dream takes courage and a bit of hope. A dream guides us, even if we haven't let ourselves bring it to consciousness. How often do we stop to ask what our dreams are? Do we even know what we want? This path is about becoming the best men we can be. It's more about who we become than what we achieve. So it inspires us to create dreams for our development as men.

When we take a few moments to reflect on the kind of men we want to be, we create reference points, or beacons, to move toward. This gives us a way to measure our actions and our choices. Do our actions take us in the direction we want to go, or do they take us off course? Are we growing into the men we want to be, or have we forgotten to follow our beacons?

In my actions today, I will keep my dreams in mind
and choose my course with confidence.

*The best inheritance a parent can give
his children is a few minutes of his time
each day.*

— *Orlando A. Battista*

As fathers, we have a strong drive to provide for our
loved ones. Many of us had fathers who were absent
from our daily lives, often because they were working
so much. Now, we also may find ourselves so dedicated
to making a living and getting ahead that we don't spend
much time with our children and all those whom we
love. We try to make up for it by giving generous gifts
or providing them with many comforts that we didn't
have ourselves.

When we get so taken up with our work, we may justify it by saying we are doing it for our families. The truth
is, nothing is as valuable as the time we spend together.
Children are certainly richer and happier with the nur-
turing presence of their father than with extra material
comforts. We always need to seek a balance. Doing well
in our careers has its place, but it isn't the most important
thing in life.

*I will keep my urge to provide for my loved ones
in balance with simply spending time with them.*

We must accept finite disappointment,
but we must never lose infinite hope.
— *Dr. Martin Luther King Jr.*

Hope and freedom and the right to dignity as a man
are very personal things for every one of us in recovery.
Regardless of our race or creed or ethnic origin, we are
alike in that we are walking this healing path out of sub-
jugation to addiction and codependency. Today is the
birthday of a heroic man, Dr. Martin Luther King Jr.,
who dedicated his life not to his own self-interest, but
to peace and the right of all people to be free. He spoke
to all people who have struggled under a yoke of pain
and trouble.

We must accept disappointments along our path. They
are inevitable. We strive hard to achieve a goal, and it
may slip from our fingers. We fall in love and lose the one
we love. In the midst of disappointment, we may doubt
whether we can handle it. But life goes on. We take our
setbacks and ask, "What do I need to learn from this?"
We don't lose sight of our long-term objective to become
the best kind of man we can be and to live in line with
our spiritual principles. That is the path to our personal
freedom and dignity.

Today, I am grateful that those who have
gone before us have shown us the path.

Failure is an event, never a person.
— *William D. Brown*

At times, we have wondered if there is hope for us. But, in fact, we can all succeed in finding peace of mind. We can all achieve self-respect. The most financially successful man may be proud of his achievement, but it doesn't satisfy him. By the same token, a major failure doesn't define a man. When we understand that our actions aren't who we are, we will not feel trapped by a failure, and we can pursue the greater prize of becoming a better man.

Today, we may be troubled by a recent failure or haunted by an old one. We are embarrassed about it and feel we have lost the high regard of our friends. This failure can propel us into greater wisdom and stronger understanding of how to live a life with value.

Today, I will take the spiritual leap away
from basing my self-esteem on what I do
toward basing it on who I am.

*Don't believe that winning is really everything.
It's more important to stand for something.
If you don't stand for something, what do you
win?*

— *Lane Kirkland*

We love competition. Many of us enjoy it both in our
recreation and in our work life. We love to run faster,
play harder, stack higher, pound more, sell more, and
produce more than our friends and co-workers. Some of
us seem almost to worship competition as a great virtue,
above other virtues such as camaraderie, teamwork, fair
play, community service, honesty, and generosity. Any
good thing can become a bad thing when it's taken to the
extreme. Intemperate competition serves our primitive,
greedy drive for power. Winning is wonderful—but it is
not the only thing we stand for.

More important than coming out ahead is coming
out with our integrity and self-respect. We preserve our
integrity by adhering to the truth as we know it, caring
for the welfare of others, and dealing fairly and honestly
both at work and at play. No win, no personal advantage
is ever worth the price of our character.

*Today, I will enjoy my competitive side while
I uphold all the other things I stand for.*

The way we see the problem is the problem.
— *Stephen R. Covey*

Many of us have a mind-set that keeps us on a treadmill. It's not for lack of effort that our lives reel out of control. We struggle to move forward. We work hard to manage the unmanageable. But with all our busy efforts, we can't see that we are continuously recycling the same problem over and over.

The solution we need may be right before our eyes. Our denial is confusing us; we don't even know we are denying anything. We cannot solve our problems alone— or even see the problems clearly from the inside. That's what friends do for us. They reflect back to us what we are missing. That's why we need to have good talks with others who have walked the same path that we are on. The strongest, most powerful men have wise advisers who show them things they don't know. They accept the role of seeker and learner because that is the way they enhance themselves.

Today, I will be open to seeing my problems
in ways I couldn't imagine on my own.

For the person who has learned to let go and
let be, nothing can ever get in the way again.
— *Meister Eckhart*

We have to learn how to let go. It doesn't come naturally until we have learned how. Letting go is a skill that comes when we see others doing it, and when we practice it. It comes when we accept that we are not completely separate individuals but part of a larger whole. Then we can turn our most vexing problems over to our Higher Power or let others deal with issues that don't belong to us. Most of us worked hard to gain control of our lives and to manage the circumstances we faced. Becoming selective about what we try to control is a very adult skill that takes time and much life experience.

When we can finally let go and stand aside from the things we don't need to manage, we get the payoff of liberation and peace of mind. Our burden is lightened, and only the things that we can handle are left.

Today, I will take every opportunity to practice
the skill of letting go and letting be.

Ninety percent of the game is half mental.
— *Yogi Berra*

A very large part of any addiction is made up of all the thinking and behavior patterns that go with it. Many addictions don't involve alcohol or other drugs at all, just the thoughts and feelings of certain behaviors. Codependency is all about unhealthy thinking. Removing addictive substances is just the start of a long process of changing ourselves mentally.

This mental transformation is the real recovery. It begins as soon as we enter this program, and we feel the rewards very quickly. We are set on a lifelong process of growth that is 90 percent mental: learning to know our feelings and express them well, relating to other people, trusting others and a Higher Power, and developing healthy attitudes.

Today, I will be aware of my mental recovery and notice how much I have already gained.

Where there is great love,
there are always wishes.
— Willa Cather

We can always think of ways to improve our intimate partnership, but usually our best ideas are for changes in our partner. We wish we had a more generous attitude from our partner; we wish we had a more agreeable partner—someone who was more fun or who would take better care of his or her health—and we want more sexual pleasure. But these ideas are the easy ones to think of. The harder and more effective ideas are those that call for changes in ourselves.

We enter into a life partnership to enjoy the relationship. We take pleasure in each other's lives, and we are on the same team. But we don't walk in the same footsteps because we all need to stand on our own as adults. Intimacy is not the merging of personalities but the bridge between separate people. Once we have our adult separateness, we can be more intimate, more loving, and more generous with each other.

Today, I will pay more attention to the
ways I can be a better partner.

In the face of uncertainty, there is
nothing wrong with hope.
— *Bernie Siegel*

Are we willing to hope? Some of us have adopted an attitude of optimism about the progress of life. We know that many things are unpredictable, but we believe we have the strength to deal with whatever happens. Others of us have chosen the opposite. We dare not hope, protecting ourselves from the hurt of disappointment. But our spiritual growth calls every one of us to believe in the possibilities for recovery and all the promises that go with it.

We need to ask ourselves, "Do I dare to hope?" That is what the Second Step challenges us to do. We simply suspend our doubts. We put them on the shelf and hold open the possibility that good things will happen. And if we don't get what we hoped for, we can deal with it. It is a choice we make.

Today, I will accept the challenge to suspend my
doubts and accept that my life can get better.

That old law about "an eye for an eye"
leaves everybody blind.
　　　　　— *Dr. Martin Luther King Jr.*

Resentment and the urge for revenge can corrode our lives. We carry these dark feelings with us, sometimes in the back of our minds and sometimes up front. Such feelings keep us living in the past and tie us to the people we resent. Our spiritual goal is to reach the point of forgiveness. It is not easy to make that transition, and it cannot be done in a phony way. A good beginning is first to accept forgiveness as a goal and then focus our efforts on a thorough and searching inventory of ourselves. Finally, we can reach the point where we simply tear up the IOU. We stop expecting repayment for past wrongs and release ourselves from carrying old resentments. We let others deal with their own God and their own conscience.

　　We reach a sense of freedom and well-being that is a great reward for forgiveness. It surprises us when our own self-esteem rises as we write off the bad debts we think others owe us.

Today, I am spending my efforts on my
own inventory because that releases me
from the burden of the past.

Journal writing is a voyage to the interior.
— *Christina Baldwin*

Many men use daily notes in a private journal as a method of meditation. It is a means to learn about themselves as they reflect with pen in hand and put uncensored thoughts down on paper. It can take many forms. Some days, a person might just make a list. It might be a prayer list: all the people he loves and all the people he is concerned about. It might be a list of the day's tasks, with notations on the spirit with which to approach them. Some guys draw pictures in their journals and say it helps them quiet their minds and deepen their understanding of a situation. Some simply record the events of the day and then reflect on how they feel about them and what they mean.

Every man in spiritual development needs a daily pattern of meditation and reflection. It should be a gentle means to respect himself, be honest with himself, and hold himself responsible for his life.

*Today, I will make notes on paper and use
my notes to interact with my thoughts.*

*Wisdom too often never comes, and so one ought
not to reject it merely because it comes late.*
— *Felix Frankfurter*

A sure sign of true growth and change is the appearance
of regret and grief that such wisdom came so late. Often,
when we deeply understand something for the first time
or make a real change that improves our lives, we wish
we had learned this a long time ago. We mourn the losses
and the pain that could have been avoided if we had only
seen the light sooner.

However, a good life always brings change and growth.
The greatest tragedy is when a man never grows and
never sees the light. We always see more clearly after we
learn something new, and the regret that accompanies
it is inevitable. With enough distance and perspective,
most of us reach the point where we say, "I wouldn't
change it if I could."

*Today, I am grateful for the wisdom I have gained,
and I will continue to seek more growth.*

You alone can do it, but you cannot do it alone.
— O. Hobart Mowrer

A guy likes to feel independent and self-sufficient. We all naturally want to feel competent and on top of our game. As we live our lives, we gain some savvy about this drive to be our own master. The young boy has a simple idea: the less he needs others, the stronger and better he will be. But the wiser, experienced man knows that a man is stronger and wiser if he is willing to accept the help that is available.

We alone can turn toward the help. We alone can decide to accept what we cannot change. We alone can open ourselves to spiritual grace and stop getting in the way of our Higher Power. The smarter man accepts the paradox that when we take our self-sufficiency too far, we become weaker. We are in the driver's seat when we decide to receive the help of others and our Higher Power.

Today, I will open myself to the help
that surrounds me.

When we see men overdoing their masculinity,
we can assume that they . . . are scared that they
aren't being manly enough.

— Frank Pittman

Masculinity is a wonderful thing. It is part of a man's inner feeling of self-esteem, and it has a wide scope. It's the feeling that we can protect and provide for ourselves, our family, and our loved ones; that we are tough when we need to be tough, standing up to difficult challenges; that we are true to our word, loving, and honorable.

As young boys, we had boyish ideas about masculinity. Boys don't know manhood until they are there. And some of us didn't have adult men we were close to; we couldn't know intimately what grown men were like. So we reached manhood almost as outsiders, still trying to fulfill our boyish ideas. We worked extra hard to fulfill the simple stereotypes of manhood. That's why we sometimes exaggerated our behavior like perpetual adolescents, always anxious about whether our masculinity was measuring up.

We don't need to be anxious about our masculinity. When we are comfortable that we are man enough, that we have arrived, there is no need to prove anything.

Today, I value my masculinity and accept myself
as a good man, just as I am.

The grand essentials of happiness are:
something to do, something to love, and
something to hope for.
— *George Washington Burnap*

A wise old man who had survived years of abuse and
hard labor in a Nazi concentration camp and lost several
loved ones to the gas chambers was asked how he could
live without getting depressed. He answered that it was
because he had a purpose in his life.

We are rebuilding our lives after the devastation of
codependency and addiction. The promises of this
recovery program tell us that we will experience the
restoration of meaning and purpose, and we will feel
like full-fledged human beings again. Now we are finding
those promises coming true every day. There is always
plenty to be depressed about. However, we have something to do, we have the love of others, and we have hope
for our future.

Today, my gratitude and purpose carry me along
with plenty to be happy about.

Can you accept the idea that some things happen for no reason, that there is randomness in the universe?

— *Rabbi Harold S. Kushner*

Whenever something bad happens to us, we ask, "Why?" We want to make sense out of our misfortune. "How could this happen to me? Why do I have to suffer this tragedy?" Sometimes we even explain our pain by saying we deserve it for being bad. It is true that many bad things have happened because of bad choices we made. But many things happen for no reason. Illness, death, and pain come into every life. There is no reasonable explanation except that these things are random.

So we accept that fact. We take reasonable precautions, drive carefully, and eat healthy foods. Most of all, we hold close to our human connections because we are all in this together. The comforting bonds of trusted friends and loved ones form the human net that holds us up through tough challenges. Within our human network, we celebrate our good times, we play and take joy in life, and we support each other when we need it.

Today, I will go beyond the question why? *and hold close to the life-giving bonds of human love.*

Man's real home is not a house
but the road, and life itself is a
journey to be walked on foot.
— *Bruce Chatwin*

We often say that one of our main needs in life is security. We want to be able to predict and control how things will play out. The problem with this view is that even when we gain more control, it doesn't generally make us feel deeply secure. If we accept security as our goal, we are soon on an endless search for more. A much wiser goal is to walk the road of life, accepting that it is always insecure. Happiness isn't found by pursuing happiness, and a sense of security isn't found by grasping for more security. They are both found by indirect means.

We find security by making peace with our insecurity and by trusting our Higher Power to care for our lives. We find happiness by taking on work that has meaning beyond ourselves.

Today, I will walk on foot the journey
that has meaning and value, and I'll accept
the insecure feelings that are part of life.

Until you make peace with who
you are, you'll never be content
with what you have.
— *Doris Mortman*

Marketers call us consumers. Ads suggest that a new car will make us happy or that when we buy our special loved one a beautiful diamond, we will really be somebody. But our awakening into a healthy, new life has nothing to do with what we own. Sure, it's fun to buy something new, but it doesn't make us happy for long. We don't define ourselves as mere consumers; rather, we are men with meaning in our lives.

When we haven't got ourselves on track, when we don't have a focus for our lives, we are easily seduced by distractions and dead-end promises. Peace of mind hasn't come easily for most of us. We had to accept some things about ourselves that we didn't want to accept. We had to learn some lessons that we couldn't easily learn at first. Now we feel like real men. We have something much better than anything we could buy with money, and no one else can take it away.

Today and every day, I restore my peace of mind
by making peace with myself.

FEBRUARY

All the art of living lies in a fine mingling
of letting go and holding on.
— *Havelock Ellis*

The wisdom that we attempt to develop in recovery is
how to balance the letting go and the holding on in our
lives. Many of us have sunk into deep holes of crisis and
despair by holding on too tightly when we needed to let
go. In other ways, perhaps, we have given up too easily
when, with faith and trust, we could have held on to
opportunities and values that seemed out of reach.

The Serenity Prayer speaks of the "wisdom to know the
difference." This power to discern between what we must
accept and what we can change creates a deep sense of
peace. It brings calm to our intimate partnership, success
to our recovery from addiction and codependency, and
greater effectiveness in our work life.

Today, I pray for the wisdom to know the
difference between what I must accept
and what I can change.

*Just by speaking I can break out of my
self-made prison.*

— June Singer

For many of us guys, words don't come easily. Maybe
we have strong feelings, strong thoughts, and important
things on our mind, but they may not translate easily into
spoken words. Even as toddlers, little boys don't generally start to speak as early as little girls do. But that is no
excuse for not working at it. Some of the most difficult
challenges produce the most creative responses.

Something magical happens when the unspoken is
finally spoken. A little of our private world is finally
known by another human being. Even more than that,
we finally know more clearly what is on our minds when
we put words to it and hear ourselves say it. We may not
even know that we are in a self-made prison of silence
until we start to break out of it. Talking—finding words
to say what is on our mind—is a big part of our healing
process.

*Today, I will talk to someone about a feeling,
a memory, or an unanswered question.*

Work for something because it is good, not just because it stands a chance to succeed.
— *Václav Havel*

We are not following the way of the mainstream. Our troubles required us to follow a path of healing and recovery that most of our community and society may not need to follow. In our society, we often hear the message that financial success, in and of itself, is a worthy goal. But on our path, we are always concerned about who we are, not just what we do. We always ask, "What is the moral good in our choices?" We don't only ask, "Will it work?" Financial success at the expense of our sobriety, serenity, or self-respect is won at far too high a price. On this path, we ask ourselves daily how we are doing on the moral scale for our lives. Do our choices and our work help create something that is good? Are we following our values, or are we just trying to get ahead? Do we treat everyone the way we want to be treated? Are we kind and respectful to the weak as well as the strong? Do we speak the truth when it is called for?

Today, I will work for what is good and leave success in the hands of my Higher Power.

What is laid down, ordered, factual is never
enough to embrace the whole truth; life always
spills over the rim of the cup.

— Boris Pasternak

We like control. We want to know what to expect. We like to think we have things figured out and know the answers. But God cannot be contained by a human definition—and life will not stay in place after we try to put it there.

When we go to work, we expect our routine to fit the normal pattern, but sometimes surprises await us. When we talk to our partner about an important topic, we expect a certain outcome—but our partner is a separate person with a separate outlook. Something happens that throws us a curve ball. When we accept that life will spill over the rim, there is no need to add our anxiety to the situation. We already know that we cannot contain it, and we learn to go with the flow. We are not in charge of everything, and we never will be. We are not responsible to keep the world on track, only to deal as best we can with what comes our way.

Today, as life spills over the rim of the cup,
I will strive to go with the flow.

To ease another's heartache is to forget one's own.
— *Abraham Lincoln*

Sometimes, in our self-centeredness, we fall into a pit of self-pity. Most of us have enough pain and heartache to feed a lifetime of self-pity if we choose to. We all have had serious losses, stressful jobs, difficult family relationships, bad breaks, and unfair dealings with others. When we start to sink into excessive self-absorption and resentment or wallow in endless negativity, we may not even recognize what we are doing. The best way to climb out of this pit is to reach out to help others who have real needs.

We can volunteer at a school to help children learn to read, or visit people in nursing homes, or help clean up a riverbank, or help a disabled person buy groceries. When we focus too much on ourselves, we become narrow and negative, but when we bring help or relief to our community, we become connected, and we have a purpose and a mission that expands our world.

Today, I will reach out to others with a helpful hand.

*In marriage, being the right person is as
important as finding the right person.*
— *Wilbert Donald Gough*

No matter how much two people love each other, no
matter how compatible they are, no matter how great
they are as lovers, they will confront matters and situations where their habits and differences will clash.
When we face a frustrating obstacle, our first impulse is
to blame the other person who doesn't fit what we want.
But our most effective way of improving our relationship
is to look beyond that first impulse and focus on what
we can change: ourselves. We need to persistently be the
best partner we know how to be. Our partner is not a
model of our own creation and was not put on this earth
just to fulfill our own image. As good partners, we try
to be good listeners and open ourselves to our beloved.
We cut our partner some slack when it's needed; we
offer forgiveness. We don't use our partner's immature
response as an excuse for us to be immature. We practice
the kind of detachment that allows our partner self-
determination. We don't try to fix or mold our beloved
to our wishes.

*Today, I will focus on being the best partner
I know how to be, regardless of what
my partner says or does.*

*You don't get harmony when everybody
sing the same note.*

— Doug Floyd

A tradition of our healing program is that we put principles above personalities. When we encounter a diverse
group of people, we may find some we feel close to right
away and others we don't particularly like. But we can
learn something valuable from any of them. Whether at
our workplace, at our place of worship, or in our Twelve
Step meetings, the diversity of a group enriches everyone. The wisdom of two or three is greater than the
closed loop in our own individual mind.

Sometimes it takes a while to arrive at that wisdom.
The Twelve Steps were created by a group of people
trying to formulate a set of suggestions that they had
found effective as a path of recovery. They disagreed
and debated over how to express that set of steps. What
they created was better than what any one of them could
have done alone. The groups we are in have the same
spiritual creative process working for our own recovery.
So we listen to the harmony created by the wisdom of
our group. Even when we don't like what we hear, we
continue the dialogue, and we grow through it.

*Today, I am grateful for the harmony created
by the diversity of people in my life.*

*An ounce of apology is worth
a pound of loneliness.*
— Joseph Joubert

The healing that comes when we make amends happens in two places. First of all, it mends the split between what we want to be and the mistake we have made. In that way, we take responsibility for our actions and reaffirm our standards for ourselves. It's a way of respecting ourselves by saying, "I believe in the standard that I didn't keep, and I will try harder next time."

The second place that healing may happen is between ourself and the person we have harmed. If it's an old mistake, with apology long overdue, the relationship may take on renewed meaning after an apology. It opens the possibility for a discussion about the friendship and its importance to each person. In other situations, an apology doesn't heal the connection and perhaps the other person isn't willing to accept it. In such a situation, we still take comfort in knowing that we have restored the split within ourselves and that we can let go of the past.

*Today, I will be sincere and quick
with my apologies.*

I never think of the future;
it comes soon enough.
—*Albert Einstein*

In our spiritual development, we learn to think about time in new ways. Many of us have come to our healing journey stuck in the past, imprisoned by fears or angers that arose years ago. We live in the past through regrets and griefs about things that can never change, and we translate them into the future with fears and foreboding. Yet we all know that life is only in the present. All we need to do is live today.

Our memories shaped us, but our development is not finished. Today, we don't have to deal with all the problems we can foresee in the future. Today, we are given a hand to play, and we can play the cards we have as we choose. With the spiritual guidance of our recovery path, we can resolve the pain of the past and our fears of the future. Our Higher Power reassures us that we will never be alone.

Today, once again, I awake into the present,
and I thank God for the chance to live this day.
I will let my Higher Power care for my fears
and regrets.

*Real friends are those who, when you've made
a fool of yourself, don't feel that you've done a
permanent job.*

— Erwin T. Randall

Friendship is one of the most important elements in a rich and joyful life. Good mental health requires that we not walk through life without one or two good friends. Many of us have been very lonely. We built invisible shields around ourselves that protected us from letting others know what we were thinking or doing, but they also separated us from the comfortable closeness of good friends. Many of us have a deep and abiding anxiety about being vulnerable to anyone, and many of us are especially guarded about getting close to other men.

In our growth as men, we are abandoning notions of perfection in ourselves and in others. We don't expect perfection, and we can expect our friends to cut us some slack when they see our mistakes and our weaknesses. True friends see in each other a complex weaving of many qualities, many experiences, and a mixture of more and less attractive qualities.

*Today, I will give my friendships the
primary place they deserve.*

Time spent laughing is time spent with the gods.
— *Japanese saying*

Many of our stories have both a dark and a light side. As we make peace with ourselves, we can take ourselves less seriously. We hang out with others who have had similar experiences, and we begin to relax. That is when the healing effects of laughter can move in. Even the worst of times has a funny side, and learning to laugh about it lightens the burden.

For a group that has lived through hard times, inside jokes are wonderful things to share. Suddenly we don't feel so alone. If my brother can laugh at the stupid things he did as a kid, I can laugh at myself too. That sense of recognition—we know what it was like, we are insiders—is another form of bonding that heals us.

Today, I will not take myself so seriously
that I cannot laugh at myself.

Growing old is not growing up.
— *Douglas Horton*

We have all met men who seemed very wise and strong for their age and other men who seemed immature and stuck in a boyish mind with an aging body. So we ask, "What is a truly grown-up man?" We think of masculine values we admire, such as strength, courage, the ability to think for oneself, wisdom, self-respect, and a sense of balance and proportion in one's actions and relationships.

Many of us have felt that we never really grasped the key to what adult masculinity was all about. We could play the role, and we could make it look pretty good, but we didn't feel in our hearts that it was ours. By walking the daily path on which we get to know ourselves from the inside, and by learning to stay true to ourselves, we develop a true self. Our true self is, by definition, no longer trapped in boyhood. We have found our inner compass, and from that comes the sterling feeling of authenticity that we wouldn't trade for anything.

Today, I am grateful for the wisdom and strength of character that is growing within.

I'm more like I am now than I ever was before.
— *Anonymous*

We are becoming more ourselves. That is our true calling. If we grow wiser and stronger with life experience, we learn to know ourselves, and we find the confidence and courage to fulfill our best self. We walk a path that is sometimes very difficult and complicated. Weighing the choices before us, we seldom have a clear, unequivocal answer. But as we know ourselves better and as we gain confidence, we gradually fulfill our true nature.

A story in the Talmud describes a man at the end of his life who fears that he will be judged by God for not living a life like Moses. The rabbi replies that God will not judge him for not being Moses, but for not being himself.

Today, I will allow myself to be more
like I am than I ever did before.

All our loves are first loves.
— *Susan Fromberg Schaeffer*

When we fall in love with someone, it is a unique thing that comes from deep within us. Any relationship is the creation of two people who open themselves to each other and share themselves beyond the usual boundaries. That is the excitement of true love. Two people give each other the keys to their private world, just as we might share the key to our home, trusting that it will be used with care and respect. This intimacy isn't usually instantaneous. It builds on experience together.

In an intimate relationship, we have the responsibility to be good stewards of the trust given to us. Looking at our partner's role is always so much easier than looking at our own, but we need to resist that easy temptation. Our first questions should always be, Do I make it safe for my partner to be open with me? Do I witness my partner's vulnerability as a trust that I do not abuse? Am I gentle and respectful with the key my partner gave me?

Today, I will be a good partner, honoring and guarding the trust I have been given.

*I imagine that God speaks to me, saying simply,
"I kept calling to you, and you did not come."
And I answer quite naturally, "I couldn't until I
knew there was nowhere else to go."*
— Florida Scott-Maxwell

We are willful. We worship guts and individual determination. A man wants to do things in the way that he devises for himself, and it may not occur to him to open himself up to a Higher Power. Yet our Higher Power is always there, calling to us.

There is a paradox in this spiritual lesson: more genuine strength and more options are in our hands when we let go of our willful, controlling attitudes. This is the secret wisdom of a man who has learned from experience. The young, unseasoned man tries to control everything and push on things that he cannot budge. The wiser, more experienced man says, "I see the limits of what is mine to change, and I can let my Higher Power take care of the things I cannot change."

*Today, I will notice those concerns that I cannot fix,
and I will let them go. Then I will focus on a few areas
where I can make a difference.*

All life is an experiment.
— *Ralph Waldo Emerson*

When we take a trip, we might plan it pretty carefully. We have expectations for what we will see, who we will visit, and what we will do. But the real purpose of a trip is to experience what happens while we follow our plans. We leave our routine of controlled and predictable days to enter another space where we will find novelty and the unpredictable. In fact, our whole life, from beginning to end, is a trip.

Once we accept that much of life is outside of our control, we can step aside. We make plans and work toward our highest goals. We take great pleasure in working toward our achievements. At the same time, the substance of life is not in controlling the outcomes but in responding to what happens along the way.

Today, I will be open and respond to
what happens while I follow my plans.

There is a basket of fresh bread on your head,
and yet you go door to door asking for crusts.
— *Rumi*

We have often tried to satisfy a deep inner hunger that
we could not describe and didn't understand. We followed the seductive call of sexual pleasures, the allure
of alcohol or other drugs, the excitement of gambling, or
even the satisfactions of being the "helpful" codependent
hero, trying to save others from their problems. These
hollow attractions never satisfied our hunger. No matter
how much we tried, they only left us more trapped in a
dead-end search and less satisfied than ever.

We find genuine satisfactions for our hunger when
we develop self-respect, form caring bonds with friends,
develop a relationship with our Higher Power, and follow
a path with heart. All of that is available to us, and we
only need to turn toward it to find it.

Today, I seek a real slice of satisfaction in life
rather than settling for crumbs.

All shall be well, and all shall be well,
and all manner of things shall be well.
— *Julian of Norwich*

Some mornings we wake with anxiety, fretting over the future or the state of our lives. Not many things we do will change the direction of events in the future. Our fears for our safety and well-being may be based more on habit than reality, and our desires for control only feed frustration.

To restore calm, we can turn to the care of our Higher Power. We do that in our deep meditation, taking a few minutes alone in a quiet, undisturbed, and safe place. We can breathe slowly and deeply, allowing the chair or the floor to hold our body as we allow our Higher Power to hold us. Repeating in our minds today's opening quote, we find calm settling over us.

Today, I accept that all will be well.

Take your work seriously but yourself lightly.
— C. W. Metcalf

As we found comfort in our addiction and codependency, we created great problems and chaos in our lives. We come into recovery with a sense of relief that we are no longer living from crisis to crisis, but we still have to deal with our persistent longing for control and security. Many of us get drawn into the same search for comfort by overindulging in work. Our job can become another addictive escape from the personal work of developing as spiritual men with deep emotional lives.

Perhaps a long-standing insecurity about our role at our workplace keeps us working longer hours than necessary, taking few vacations, or even working seven days a week. Perhaps a deep feeling of guilt and shame drives us into unending work, as if we could redeem ourselves by working harder and longer. No matter how virtuous or successful we are at our job, it will only cover these underlying fears, never resolve them. Only by facing our insecurities and guilts directly will we ever grow spiritually.

Today, I will take time to play, to spend time in my relationships, and perhaps just to loaf.

*We must learn to reawaken and keep ourselves
awake, not by mechanical aids, but by an infinite
expectation of the dawn.*

— *Henry David Thoreau*

The wisdom of hope in the face of trouble is a fundamental principle of the spiritual path. We expect to have problems, and we've already come through many of them. Our problems haven't dashed our hopes. Our awakening in the spiritual life means that even in the darkest night, we expect that dawn always comes. We have problems, we respond to them, and things get better.

Our spirituality shows us how to have serenity in the face of risk. We accept the darkness because it is inevitable, but we are not defeated by it. We rise above it with our trust in our Higher Power to lead us toward the inevitable light.

*Today, my awakening means I trust in a
Higher Power to lead me to a better future.*

Feeling gratitude and not expressing it is like
wrapping a present and not giving it.
— William Arthur Ward

We could never have arrived at this point in our lives without the help of a lot of other people. It has been said that we stand on the shoulders of all those who have gone before us. But we've also benefited from many people in our lives who were kind, who believed in us when we didn't believe very strongly in ourselves. We've benefited from the anonymous multitude of men and women who shone a light on the path to recovery. Sometimes we know within our hearts that someone made a big difference to us, but it is hard to admit it to that person. We may even develop a grudging attitude toward people who have helped us because we are stingy about giving them any credit.

The surprising thing about gratitude is that the more we express it, the larger it grows. As grown men, we all have a mountain of things and people to be thankful for. If we don't express gratitude, our withholding diminishes us. The more we say it and give it away, the bigger and stronger we feel.

Today, I will thank someone who has helped me.

> *If you do not make it empty,*
> *how will you fill it up again?*
> — *Neem Karoli Baba*

There is a myth that most men believe: we should always be on top of any situation, and we shouldn't show weakness or vulnerability. But the myth creates a paradox, because if we are never vulnerable, we are never open to learning anything new. How can we learn anything new if we have to look as if we already know the answers? So we become weaker while trying to appear strong.

It is said that nothing can be added to a vessel that is already full. A truly strong, wise man is willing to doubt, and willing to empty himself of his preconceived ideas so that he continues to learn and grow.

Today, I will not concern myself with being right.
Instead, I will strive to have an open mind.

Conscience is God's presence in man.
— *Emanuel Swedenborg*

As we mature, our conscience grows, and vice versa. We follow a principle that directs us to promptly admit when we are wrong. That practical piece of guidance is the most effective way to become bigger, stronger men. To follow it, we must abandon our ego's desire to always be right. We must abandon the thought that we are belittled by such an admission.

In this process of becoming better men, we open ourselves and allow God to enter. We let God speak to us and through us by humbly accepting that we don't always have to be right. The higher principles of honesty and responsibility are our guides, and we don't expect perfection from ourselves. In that way, we become more honest with ourselves and with our friends.

*Today, I will be open to the truth that
my Higher Power speaks within me.*

Woe to the man so possessed that
he thinks he possesses God!
— Martin Buber

When we first set out on this spiritual path, we learn
that a relationship with "God *as we understood Him*" is
a requirement for healing. So many of us think that we
have to begin by defining our personal understanding of
God. This is indeed a good question for us to think about.
Yet the greatest thinkers, beginning in the most ancient
times, have told us that God is truly beyond definition.
In the oldest Judeo-Christian history, even the name of
God could not be pronounced.

It is one thing to ask where we find our spiritual
renewal. It is another thing to try to invent it. And as
soon as we think we have the answer, as soon as we
believe we hold the true definition of God, we may be
off the spiritual path. In the end, the true spiritual path is
always a learning process and has a good deal of mystery.

Today, I turn my life over to God,
Who I can never fully understand.

Why not go out on a limb?
Isn't that where the fruit is?
— Frank Scully

From the day we are born, our lives are risky. We may be intimidated by a task or a challenge before us. Working on some of the Twelve Steps is a risk. When we face these challenges, we can draw courage from looking at other risks we have taken and perhaps even enjoyed. For instance, most sports are exciting because they play on the possibility of winning or losing. Falling in love is a risk. Climbing a mountain is a risk. Building something with our hands is a risk. Yet we enjoy the pleasure of stepping into these risks. Taking a risk makes us feel alive.

When we think about these enjoyable adventures, where risks add to the excitement, we can use that feeling as a model for approaching the risks that we avoid. Perhaps we need to talk to our spouse or partner about something that is hard to say. Perhaps we need to make amends to someone for a past wrong, and we don't know how we will be received. Perhaps our greatest challenge is to subdue our own will for something and give it over to the care of our Higher Power.

Today, I will recall the risks that make me
feel alive and move forward with those things
I have been avoiding.

*To remain whole, be twisted. To become straight,
let yourself be bent. To become full, be hollow.*
— *Lao Tzu*

The first three Steps of our Twelve Step program make
the ancient spiritual wisdom real in our lives. First, we
give in to the fact that we are powerless in a very real
way in our lives. Then we open ourselves to the healing
that comes not of our own making but from our Higher
Power.

We live the paradox of spiritual development. Every
day that we admit the ways in which we are powerless,
and every day that we live in true humility, we become
stronger, wiser men. Although we aren't totally powerless, there are some things we can never control. Owning
up to that truth makes us stronger. Having the respect
that is inherent in humility makes us grow in wisdom.

*Today, I am grateful for the spiritual guidance
I am learning in this program.*

*You may be disappointed if you fail, but
you are doomed if you don't try.*
— Beverly Sills

Anyone who has achieved great things has also faced failure. Learning how to deal with disappointment and loss is a first step in moving forward in life. We cannot live happily and well if we have not learned how to handle failure. Some of us were traumatized by terrible events in our past and reacted by seeking only security and control. Some of us were so ashamed and guilty about our out-of-control addiction and codependency that in recovery we have avoided all risk.

On the healing path, we strive to be calm. Even when life brings disappointment, we can cope because our self-esteem doesn't have to be at risk. We can feel good about ourselves when we go up to bat and give our best swing, even if we strike out. We may have tried to avoid losses by staying out of the game completely. But when we join the game and play our best, we feel better about ourselves; we enjoy life more and continue to grow. That is the only way we will find the joy of success.

*Today, I will step up to bat and
give life my best swing.*

*No man who sets out to achieve total masculinity
can ever be man enough.*

— Frank Pittman

Some people attack the whole idea of masculinity as a
problem in the world. They claim it is the cause of wars,
abuse, and the reckless pursuit of power. As grown-up
men, we know that those people are speaking of masculinity that has not grown up. Boys trying to be men take
the appearance of masculinity to extremes. They look at
masculinity from the outside: they know they have not
yet achieved it, so they try to imitate it. As adult men,
we have come to terms with ourselves and with life. We
carry the values of strength and protection of those we
love, and we value our virility for all its pleasures. We also
know from life experience that all men are complex; we
don't need to hide our vulnerability in order to be strong.

We don't have to worry about our masculinity, because
that is a given. We don't have to prove it to ourselves or
anyone else. From that grown-up perspective, we accept
ourselves as both strong and gentle, capable both of fighting for what we believe in and yielding to others when
that's what's called for.

*Today, I accept that I have nothing to prove about
being a man, and I can grow in all the ways
any adult needs to continue to grow.*

*It is only with the heart that one can see rightly;
what is essential is invisible to the eye.*
— *Antoine de Saint-Exupéry*

We are surrounded by cynical attitudes and mistrust.
We may carry a large ring of keys that symbolize all the
guards we maintain as part of ordinary daily life. It is
hard for us to develop a vision from our hearts amidst
all this wariness. Indeed, we are trying to move beyond
the scorn and contempt of the mainstream world. What
we pursue is an alternative and wiser way.

What the heart can see is the deeper man in the person
next to us. Sometimes, with our hearts, we see good as
well as bad inside ourselves and others. We can see a
future developing for our children and all the young
people around us. Instead of protecting only ourselves,
we also see opportunities to help others and to take on
worthwhile projects that benefit our communities; we
escape the narrow confines of our self-centeredness.
When we exercise our vision, it grows stronger every
day, and we see more.

*Today, I will open my heart to see beyond
my personal walls and into the true nature
of those around me.*

MARCH

Every man I meet is in some way my superior.
— *Ralph Waldo Emerson*

When we are in a competitive frame of mind, we compare ourselves to those around us. We may conclude that we are better in some ways and worse in other ways. Perhaps the darkest part of our personality takes pleasure in looking down on others. Some of us feel inferior to almost everyone.

The true measure of a man has many dimensions. Is he physically strong, mentally determined, generous, a good father, a good partner, courageous, honest, wise, warm-hearted, responsible for himself, intelligent, musically talented, athletically gifted, a good communicator? Good qualities are countless. No one has all of them— and sometimes too much of a good thing is a bad thing. When we reach the place where we accept ourselves and make peace with who we are, we can comfortably accept everyone else, knowing that their strengths and weaknesses add up in different ways, and everyone deserves basic human respect.

Today, I will practice respect for everyone I meet.

*I visualize the course nine or ten times every
night as I'm going to sleep. By race day, I've run
the course a hundred times in my head.*
— A. J. Kitt, Olympic skier

World-class athletes reach the pinnacle of performance
by intense work and dedication. No one doubts their
priorities. They practice for hours every day, endure the
pain of pushing the body to the limit, and develop the
mind psychologically to be ready to respond in a split
second. We can use that same model for our healing
recovery program. We need to put our recovery above all
else—because without that, we have nothing. We need
to accept the pain that comes with facing ourselves and
our truth, because on the other side of the pain is peace
of mind. And we can develop our self-image as recovering men in the care of our Higher Power, succeeding as
we meet the challenges of our days.

A very helpful daily practice is to visualize ourselves
in a quiet place, feeling well, content, and safe. Staying
with this image for fifteen minutes or so, just enjoying
its peace, creates a sense of strength and serenity for the
next few hours or for the rest of the day.

*Today, I know my first priority is recovery, and I can
picture myself feeling content in a quiet setting.*

Love is an ideal thing, marriage is a real thing;
a confusion of the real with the ideal never goes
unpunished.

— *Johann Wolfgang von Goethe*

When two people decide to become life partners, they'll need to make adjustments. These include moving from feelings of pleasure and excitement to managing the more practical aspects of daily life. In that interdependent life, we have to carry our share of the work. Sometimes we may feel let down; sometimes our partner will feel let down by us. We have to deal with differences and learn how to respect them while maintaining the connection.

When we enter the realm of partnership, while we may struggle and feel frustrated at times, we come to know each other more deeply—and we become more vulnerable. Our first task is to be sure that our partner is in good hands with us. That means we don't willingly hurt our partner, and we don't use abusive or threatening words. We also expect that our own vulnerability and trust will be handled with care by our partner. With these rules in place, our intimacy continues to deepen through the practical details of our lives.

Today, I accept the real world
of daily life in my love life.

Great opportunities to help others seldom come,
but small ones surround us every day.
— *Sally Koch*

From its earliest days, the Twelve Step program began with the Twelfth Step. When a certain recovering man in Ohio was tentatively making his way into sobriety, day by day, he quickly realized that his progress depended on telling his story to other suffering alcoholics. He realized that by helping others, he was helping himself stay sober.

A fundamental rule of good mental health is to be helpful to others. We can do that by telling our story: where we were and how far we have come. But helpfulness is an attitude. We can cultivate this attitude, looking for ways to be helpful while not taking on a caretaking role. Generosity of spirit in all our dealings with others, without looking for anything in return, creates a feeling of connection with others. Helping others can also dispel depression and self-pity.

Today, I will look for ways to be
helpful and generous to others.

I just keep goin' up there and swingin' at 'em.
— *Babe Ruth*

Even Babe Ruth had his share of strikeouts. On this recovery path, relapse is always a possibility, and we need to learn how to avoid it—and how to deal with it if it happens. What do many guys feel first when they relapse? Shame. This feeling may be unavoidable, but we do best if we don't stay there long. It is not what we deserve to feel, and it weakens us. After a relapse, the first productive thing to do is tell our recovery group and sponsor. When we do that, we expose our addictive and codependent side. That side may want to stay hidden and secret, but our recovery requires that we shine the light of day on it. The second thing to do is ask ourselves what we can learn from this relapse. If we can learn the lessons it has to teach us, it is no longer a deficit but an asset that strengthens our healing. Some relapses happen when we fail to take care of ourselves; we get too worn out, too depleted, too needy. Some happen because we associate with others who support our addictive impulses. But after a strikeout we can still go up there and swing at 'em again.

Today, I know once again that I am powerless over my addiction and my codependency.

Listen, or thy tongue will keep thee deaf.
— *Native American proverb*

Much of what we learn on this path comes from others also making their way. We go to meetings and listen to their reflections and their stories and we think, "That's like me." When neighbors or friends at work tell us about their lives, we often gain insight about our own. Sometimes we think, "I guess I didn't have it so bad." By being a good listener, we may get encouragement to stay on the path.

It's an honor to have others disclose to us what they have been through. And it's a trust that we ought to respect. Listening with an open heart isn't always easy. It doesn't mean that we simply sit there while others talk. It means that we engage actively to perceive what they are telling us and to understand how they came to feel and think as they do. When we put our ego aside, we stop thinking about what we will say in response; we stop trying to offer helpful advice or a better answer. We just take in what they are trying to tell us.

Today, I will actively engage as a good listener.

*One has to go beyond the pairs of opposites
to find the real source.*

— Joseph Campbell

We have the habit of seeing things in absolute terms, as either black or white, all or nothing, good or evil. Perhaps we find comfort in the simplicity of a clear and total answer. But this habit leads us down many mistaken paths. We might think, "Since I made a mistake I must be a bad person." Or perhaps, "After he insulted me, I can never be his friend."

Rarely do we find truth at the extremes. Within our complex human nature, we must deal with many different drives and forces. We feel generous and giving, and we feel selfish. We want to be helpful and caring, but sometimes we get so angry we feel like hurting someone. When we can accept the mixture of drives within ourselves, we can learn to manage them as good and mature men. Sometimes we need to make repairs after we break our own rules. Sometimes we say something that we regret, and we need to stay in the dialogue to reach a new understanding. When we can accept our own complexity, we become much more understanding of the same in others.

*Today, I will look for the middle ground
between extremes.*

To be without some of the things you want
is an indispensable part of happiness.
— Bertrand Russell

We learn, as we make peace with ourselves, that we have enough. Our old mind became anxious if we thought we needed something we could not have. We feared we would not be safe or comfortable, and we sought security in the comfort of things. Like the rush to the food market before a storm, the prospect of scarcity haunted us, and we got anxious.

On the spiritual path we learn to say, "I have enough. I will not have more to deal with than I can handle. All will be well. I am in the care of my Higher Power." We can't say it once and have it settled. Just as we practice healthy eating habits or safe driving, this is called *spiritual practice* because we continue doing it. We often forget the reassurance, and we need to keep returning to it. Something changes inside when we accept that we can be at peace, and we can be happy, even when we don't have everything we want.

Today, I live with satisfaction that I have enough.

*Courage doesn't always roar. Sometimes courage
is that little voice at the end of the day that says:
"I'll try again tomorrow."*

— *Anne Hunninghake*

A key quality that distinguishes successful athletes,
or top-notch performers in any field, is the way they
respond to their bad days. Everyone has good days
and bad days, and the good ones are certainly easier to
handle. But do we allow the bad ones to throw us off our
course? Are we so shaken by our mistakes or troubles
that we lose our focus on our goals?

Adult development is a process; it's never an end
goal that we reach and hold. Our healing and recovery
include preparing ourselves to respond well to the bad
days. We can do that by keeping our eye on the big picture, knowing that however bad things may seem at the
moment, they will change. We learn to reach deep into
our spiritual center for the courage to stay focused in the
midst of our hardest days. We don't have to do it alone.
We have the spiritual support of our Higher Power and
the companionship of our friends to keep us on the path.

*Today, I will stay in touch with my spiritual center
to find the courage for another day.*

At the heart of the simple life is an emphasis
on harmonious and purposeful living.
— *Duane Elgin*

At some point, we all complain about the fast pace and complexity of modern life. We rush the kids to school or day care, and when we get to work, we practice multitasking, trying to be more efficient and productive. Driving home from work, we catch up on some phone calls. But somehow, as busy as we are, we are never led to that point of completion with calm and quiet—only to more busyness.

To have a simpler life, we have to consciously choose it. Busily running around and embracing more tasks does not open the door to simplicity. We can decide not to be frantic and scattered in our daily tasks. Instead, we can be attentive, present in the moment, and focused on the one thing that is before us. Being in harmony with our surroundings is at least as important as efficiency. When we choose to push back against the hectic pace and move toward simplicity and harmony, we think more clearly, we know ourselves better, we make better choices, our physical health is stronger, and maybe we are actually more productive.

Today, I will choose simplicity and harmony.

*Never doubt that a small group of thought-
ful, committed citizens can change the world;
indeed, it's the only thing that ever has.*
— Margaret Mead

The pessimists and the naysayers believe that the future is bleak. Storm clouds are always present somewhere, they say, leading things inexorably to the worse. Yet our own recovery and our restored lives are living proof that growth and improvement are always possible. We know how bad things felt in our own lives and how much better they have now become. Our own experience is all we need to give us hope.

When a couple of guys in Ohio first got together to find a path out of alcoholism and despair, they started the Twelve Step recovery program that has brought hope and transformation to millions. When so many around them were hopelessly caught in the grip of alcoholism, these guys dared to hope that they could be restored to sanity. They changed the world.

On this day, perhaps we see danger looming. We may despair about a relationship, or worry about a friend or loved one. But if we care, and if we keep the faith, we know that things can change for the better.

*Today, I will carry the knowledge that a Power
greater than ourselves can restore us.*

Fear will assault us, but we will not be afraid.
— *Rabbi Harold S. Kushner*

Worry and concern are among our biggest challenges as we follow our paths. Nothing can finally and completely shield us from the vulnerabilities and unknowns. We may be haunted by experiences from our past when our safety and security were stripped away. In the back of our minds, we carry images of chaotic moments. Now we are seeking something called peace of mind and serenity—but we have to find a way to do that in the face of universal insecurity.

Many of us feel innocent about our controlling behavior because we think we are only trying to make everyone safe and secure. The practice of a good life requires us to learn attitudes and understandings that help us let go of fear when it assaults us. This means that we turn to our spiritual foundation, knowing that we are never alone and that even though we cannot control everything, the forces of a Power greater than ourselves also move in our best interest. We can quiet our minds by cultivating a close relationship with our Higher Power.

Today, I will walk my path, knowing that
my Higher Power is beside me.

Being defeated is often a temporary condition.
Giving up is what makes it permanent.
— *Marilyn vos Savant*

Powerlessness and helplessness are two very different things. When we encounter something that we cannot change and we pray to accept its truth, we gain the wisdom of powerlessness. The new reality that follows acceptance may transform us or teach us a new lesson. Sometimes, however, we encounter something that can be changed, yet the challenge seems overwhelming. It's natural to feel intimidated when facing a high mountain before us. We feel like running away or pretending it isn't there, or we just want to lie down and give up. When we actually give in to those feelings and hide from the hard task, we choose helplessness, and nothing gets better.

Challenges rise up in everyone's path. So we look squarely into the eye of the challenge before us today. We get to know its dimensions as well as we can see them. It may seem either daunting or small. We can choose to take one specific action that will move us a little closer to our goal. Just one small action keeps us from the condition of helplessness, of giving up.

Today, I will do what I can in this
one day, and it will be progress.

He knows not his own strength
that hath not met adversity.
— Ben Jonson

A man who has never had difficult times, lived through the pain of loss, or confronted a big mistake has nothing to fall back on. In getting through our hard times, we learn to know ourselves better. We find our strong sides and our weaknesses. And in the end, as difficult as some adversity can be, we have survived—and survival itself is a good thing.

Some of us are in the midst of difficult times today. From this spot, we may not be able to see where the road leads next. We are fearful about how things will turn out. In the spiritual life, we accept that we cannot know where this path leads, or even what is around the next bend, but we never have to be alone. Because we will stay true to ourselves and do what is honest and fair, we can take risks to make things better.

Today, I will rely on my Higher Power and my
friends as my guide through difficult times.

I imagine one of the reasons people cling
to their hates so stubbornly is because they
sense, once hate is gone, they will be forced
to deal with pain.

— James Baldwin

Why do we hold on to our resentments and our hates?
They poison our personality and keep us in a negative
state of mind. Maybe some of us don't know any better
or don't realize we have any other options. Probably some
of us don't want to face the feelings we have underneath.
Hate and resentment are secondary emotions. They
cover more primary feelings such as hurt, grief, empti-
ness, and low self-worth.

So we face our true feelings and let go of hate and
resentment. This is painful at first. Our egos want to
hold on to the protection, claiming we are entitled to
feel so negative. We justify these feelings, but they only
keep us stuck. When we get honest with ourselves about
our underlying feelings, we can start changing what we
can change. Our burden is lightened, and we are free to
move on with our lives.

Today, I will face my primary feelings
and let go of my negativity.

*Human beings love to be right. When a person
is willing to give up being right, a whole world
of possibilities opens up.*

— Pete Salmansohn

We naturally want others to respect us. Our urge to be right, even when we are wrong, gets us into many jams. We have seen others laughed at for their mistakes, and we ourselves have done some of the laughing. Maybe we have been the target of ridicule for not knowing the right answer or the right way to do something.

A grown-up man has lived enough and seen enough to know that honest mistakes are inevitable; indeed, they are lessons. In fact, the only way we learn is by trying out an idea, testing a new method. When we are open to seeing reality as it is, rather than blindly defending our rightness, we get wiser.

As grown men, we voice our ideas honestly, and we listen to others. We don't have to push our ideas as right. We can take on the attitude of dignity and open-mindedness, seeking the best answer and always learning.

*Today, I will consciously set aside my drive to
always be right so that I can continue to learn.*

A "no" uttered from the deepest conviction is
better and greater than a "yes" merely uttered
to please, or what is worse, to avoid trouble.
— *Mahatma Gandhi*

We don't like to make anyone unhappy with us. We don't like to hurt anyone's feelings. We feel best when others tell us they like what we do. And we have the idea that we are strong enough to put aside our own wishes and feelings when others have strong desires. In our denial, we tell ourselves, "I can handle it." We have even violated our sense of what is right because someone else insisted.

Many a man has gotten himself into serious problems because he didn't muster the courage to say no at critical times. In sexual situations, we said, "I couldn't hurt her feelings." In work situations, we said, "I'm only doing it the way everyone else does it." Within our families, we said, "I don't want to cause an uproar." But now, with our good values and our good intuition, we can find the strength to stand up for what we believe. We have our honor and our self-respect for staying honest.

Today, I will speak my honest truth,
not to be right but to be true to myself.

Who forces time is pushed back by time;
who yields to time finds time on his side.
— *The Talmud*

We are impatient for results. Upon entering a program of recovery, going without a drink or giving up other addictive behaviors for more than a day or a week seems like a huge challenge. When we see friends in recovery with several years of sobriety, we can't imagine achieving that. Future time can seem like a mountain. Our attitude shifts when we see time not as a challenge that we must overcome, but as our friend, working for us. Time is more like a lake that we swim in. It holds us up and carries us along.

One day at a time, we live only in this present moment. We live more fully when we are present to this moment, yielding to what time will do, letting go of frets and worries about the future.

On this day, I will be alive
and aware of my experience.

Next time you're feeling at odds with yourself,
make a list of your good qualities . . . things
like generosity and patience and thrift. It will
surprise you to discover how nice you really are.
— *Audrey Corn*

Some days we just feel out of sorts and down on ourselves. In this program, we place great importance
on self-inventories. We confront our defects and our
wrongs, and we make lists of them to hold ourselves
responsible. Any good inventory counts both assets and
liabilities. On a day when we feel burdened with guilt or
weakness, we ought to remind ourselves of the best of
who we are. Remember good deeds that we have done.
Remember what we do well, and don't minimize those
assets. If we are going to build on our strengths, we have
to see them for what they are.

Our attitude toward ourselves and toward life is partly
a matter of mental discipline. It does no good for anyone
if we sit passively in our negativity. We can learn to affirm
that we are children of creation, and we have a right to
be here. In spite of our imperfections, we are a force
for good.

Today, I will carry in my thoughts
some of my good qualities.

We have ever more perfect eyes in a world
in which there is always more to see.
— *Pierre Teilhard de Chardin*

Today's quotation could be seen as one of the promises
of recovery. When we enter into a program of spiritual
and emotional renewal, we choose to become honest
with ourselves. In the process, our eyes begin to see
more clearly, and we become aware of the many ways
we have been dishonest with ourselves. Each new bit
of self-honesty builds the base for more insight and an
ever-sharper understanding of ourselves and our world.
When we started with our decision to be honest, we
could never have predicted what we would find down
the path.

We first surrender to the truth as we know it, and this
clarity about ourselves and the world grows into great
insight. The world opens up for us, and we find ever
more to see and learn. We feel very alive every moment.

Today, I continue my commitment
to see the truth wherever I find it.

*You can cut all the flowers but you
can't keep spring from coming.*
— *Pablo Neruda*

Our lives are always enriched when we get closer to
nature. In springtime, just going for a walk around the
block can lift our spirits. Sometimes we feel blue, or
we are overwhelmed with emotions that are painful or
frightening. Even when our feelings are based on real
concerns, we need to manage them in order to confront
difficult situations. One of the best things we can do for
ourselves is to get outside.

Putting ourselves under the open sky, feeling the
weather against our skin, and moving our muscles in a
walk or a run changes our emotions and relieves tension.
During the worst of times, we may have a hard time
making ourselves go out and move. But when we do, we
always feel better. Spring is nature's promise that nothing
is forever. Change and new life are sure to come.

*Today, I welcome spring as the metaphor that life
is constantly being renewed and refreshed.*

If you treat every situation as a life-and-death matter, you'll die a lot of times.

— *Dean Smith*

We have lived through many crises. Many of us grew up in situations that were chaotic and filled with turmoil. We felt constantly on the edge of catastrophe and needed to be ever-vigilant to avoid it. We lost our ability to sift and screen what was genuinely in need of our attention and what we could just turn over to the work of the universe.

The spiritual part of recovery promises that we can rest in the care and security of a Higher Power. Not every situation has to automatically go to the top of our priority list of things to fix. Even if this is a random universe, forces are always in play to keep things working and put things in order. Often our anxiety and our attempts to fix things only get in the way of a good solution. So we can relax and trust that if we reserve our energy for the things we can improve, this change within ourselves will make the world a better place.

Today, I will be more discerning about what really is critical and try to stay out of the way of my Higher Power.

*Remember that not getting what you want
is sometimes a stroke of good luck.*
— H. Jackson Brown Jr.

Managing desires is one of the most crucial elements of being an adult. Children want many things that aren't good for them, and their impulses can often get them into trouble. They need loving, caring adults to protect them from the harm that can come from getting what they want. As adults, our spiritual development includes learning how to regard our desires and how to manage them. On the one hand, it isn't healthy to become so controlled and repressed that we never let ourselves have fun, and on the other hand, we know that indulging every desire will kill us.

Sometimes we want something very badly and when we don't get it, we feel desperate or very disappointed. However, life continuously points us in directions we hadn't expected. Disappointment can serve to reset our lives. Not getting our desires, if we keep our eyes open, points us in directions that can be better than what we had imagined for ourselves.

*Today, I will be open to the new directions
that life points me toward.*

Getting angry can sometimes be like leaping into a wonderfully responsive sports car, gunning the motor, taking off at high speed and then discovering the brakes are out of order.

— Maggie Scarf

Anger can multiply our difficulties in many situations. All of us can look back and remember times when we only made our problems worse because we stepped on the gas and lost all ability to use the brakes. Our masculine roles sometimes glorify aggression for its own sake. We are proud of how aggressive we can be, and we may confuse it with anger.

Now we are growing into more adult manhood. We are learning to manage our feelings and use them well. This doesn't happen overnight. We would do well to recall how energized we have felt when we let our anger fly and how much we loved that energy at the moment. Only later did we face the damage we caused. Saying we are sorry isn't enough; we must also be willing to take on the harder task of changing our behavior. When we accept that we love the power and the energy of our anger and aggression, we can begin to rein it in and take charge of it rather than be ruled by it.

Today, I will not indulge in the pleasure of anger allowed to run wild.

My father didn't tell me how to live;
he lived, and let me watch him do it.
— *Clarence Budington Kelland*

The most powerful teaching is done by example. We all have strong feelings about our fathers and what we learned or didn't learn from them. Some of us have fathers who stand as great examples of how we would like to live. Some of us have fathers who are negative examples that we want to avoid. Some of us never got to know our fathers. For most of us, it is a complicated mixture of all those things.

Now, as we continue to grow and change in adulthood, we are faced with growing beyond what our parents taught us, both the good and the bad. We need to forge ahead and become our own growing version of adult men. There are many men who can serve as examples to us; some of them were in our past, and some of them are now friends and mentors. Sometimes the example is unconscious. It is always helpful to notice who we admire, who sets an example that we would like to follow. Take the best of what they have to offer and leave the rest.

Today, I am grateful for what I received
from my father and from all the other men
who have set examples in my life.

*Tuning and training the mind as an athlete tunes
and trains his body is one of the primary aims of
all forms of meditation.*

— *Lawrence LeShan*

The longer we follow the Steps that guide our path, the
more we grow as men. We all know the value of getting
in shape and staying in shape physically. Working out
brings results very quickly, and if we are working on
our golf game or improving our running time, the more
we practice, the more progress we make. We can attend
to our minds in the same way. One difference between
these kinds of development is that age is on our side as
we train our minds. No aging process can diminish the
kind of person we are.

Spiritual growth moves forward by paying attention
to it and by devoting some time every day to prayer and
meditation. Conscious contact with our Higher Power,
sitting quietly for a few minutes every day, influences
us throughout the day in the background of our minds.

*Today, I will quietly open my mind
to the deep truths and allow them
to train my thoughts.*

*Somewhere in each of us we're a mixture
of light and of darkness, of love and of hate,
of trust and of fear.*

— Jean Vanier

We have gone to extremes in our lives. We've got a penchant for seeing things as all or nothing, black or white. A real man is made up of mixtures and blends, but we tend to think of ourselves as either the greatest or the worst, the smartest or the dullest.

In our progress toward recovery, we see that we are not separate from other people. We are like all people. As we learn to know ourselves, we see parts that we like and parts that appall us. But honesty with ourselves trumps any other defect. So in the very act of admitting a defect, we lay the foundation for accepting ourselves.

*Today, I will be honest with myself about
my many facets and accept the mixture
as truly human.*

My history is a gift, like my body—
it's what I am made of.
— *Shawnee Undell*

If our bodies are the hardware, our histories are part of the software. We sometimes cringe when we look back at things we did or things that happened. We are tempted to indulge in magical thinking, hoping to turn back the clock and relive events to make them turn out differently. But our experiences, good and bad, are the stuff that teaches what we need to learn. When we look back, we cannot change what happened. History is history. But we did choose what we made of what happened, and we can still choose: that is always open to revision. Even today, we can deepen and improve on how we respond to what happened.

Our growth continues into the present and for as long as we live.

Today, I am responding constructively
to what has happened in my history.

The true name of eternity is today.
— *Philo*

Today is the only focus for our recovery. When we look into the future, we worry. What if I slip when temptations mount at some future time? What if I get lost and confused and fall back into my codependency?

The only real truth is how we live today. The sun will come up tomorrow, and we will live the new day as we do this day, in the present moment, staying true to ourselves. Tomorrow's problems are only in our imagination. What are we doing today?

Eternity is beyond time. It is at hand.

Today, I am mindful of my immediate moment.

*The last of the human freedoms is to
choose one's attitude in any given set
of circumstances.*

— Viktor Frankl

Today's quotation was written by a man who survived
a Nazi death camp. His philosophy was formed in the
crucible of the bleakest kind of situation, in prison with
hard labor, little food, and no comforts, where everyone
was worked until they died. One could say Frankl had no
choices remaining, but he didn't accept that. He speaks
to all of us as we deal with our own particular circumstances. When we gain the wisdom of powerlessness,
we know that we often have little choice about what happens, but we have choices about the attitudes we adopt.

When we face a tough situation on the job, we can
still choose to give our best. When family problems
seem overwhelming, we may not be able to fix them all
alone, but we have options to be the best partner, the best
father, or the best son that we know how to be. And when
we turn our lives and our will over to the care of a Higher
Power, we can choose to be hopeful for the future.

*Today, I choose to have a constructive attitude
in all that I am dealing with.*

Solitude is important to man. . . . It is his refuge when the very foundations of his life are being shaken by disastrous events.

— *Margaret E. Mulac*

In the modern world, it's much easier to pursue the busy hectic life of work and responsibilities than to pursue solitude. Even though we have often felt very alone, we have been afraid to be alone with ourselves. But it is in those quiet moments alone that we honestly meet ourselves and lay the groundwork to learn from our experiences.

When we are so busy with our intense daily lives, perhaps dealing with crises, and do not take any quiet time for ourselves, we cannot look at where we are going, and we cannot learn from all that experience. Just a few minutes to simply let ourselves breathe is a valuable gem of time set aside that enriches the whole day.

My quiet moments of solitude are precious elements in my growing sobriety.

APRIL

*Be patient toward all that is unsolved in
your heart and try to love the questions
themselves.*

— *Rainer Maria Rilke*

We carry problems and discrepancies within us, quandaries that are not easily answered—and we have bigger questions about life and the world. Why did I act as I did in my younger years? Can my life partnership be happy again? How should I handle a secret that I carry? What is this thing we call Higher Power and God?

We are on a journey, and in some ways this journey is a quest for answers. The questions give energy and direction to our seeking. We cannot expect to get quick or easy answers. And some questions will always remain just that: questions. But we can learn to be patient with ourselves, tolerant of our incompleteness, and always curious about how it will all turn out.

*Today, I will practice patience with myself
and embrace my unsolved questions as
crucial elements in my quest.*

*Once the game is over, the king and the
pawn go back into the same box.*
— *Italian saying*

We may feel that we are less than other men, or greater
than someone else, but in the big picture, we are all
created equal. In our low self-esteem, we may feel less
worthy than the next guy. Some of us have built defenses
against our shame and guilt by thinking we are superior,
but that is still the flip side of the shame coin. No matter
what we have done, no matter what has happened to us,
no matter what anyone else says, our behavior and our
experiences are not the same as who we are.

The way to step out of the shame and blame problem
with our self-esteem is to accept our humility. The word
humility has the same root as *human* and *humus*. We all
are of the earth. Humility is in contrast with humiliation,
however. Humility helps us outgrow our self-absorption
and see our connection with all people. In recovery, no
matter what our social status is, we all deal with addiction and codependency. Our humility shows us how to
be respectful of everyone, including ourselves.

*Today, I accept my humility and equality
with all other people.*

Loneliness is . . . when you wish someone else was there, and solitude is when you enjoy being alone.

— *Jonathan Van Ness*

This path is an alternative to the lifestyles portrayed by Hollywood and the popular media. It is about finding happiness on a deeper level than immediate gratification. It is about a bigger, fuller kind of happiness than we can find in a new car or an erotic one-night stand. No hit sitcom or drama shows the way. No commercial touts the joy that can be found in peace of mind.

Solitude is quiet. It is not loneliness, and it is not neediness. Solitude is the way we meet ourselves; it is the place where we first get honest and finally accept the truths we have been avoiding. It is the place where we are alone with God. Many of us don't know how to be alone. We have never actually accepted our own companionship or taken on the role of self-care. We can start by taking a few minutes of quiet, in a room or on a park bench. In that quiet moment, we might simply make a list of what we are grateful for, or speak to God about what we want help with. In solitude, we learn to reach down into our inner well of knowing, where we find guidance.

Today, I will seek the solitude that transforms my life.

When you teach your son,
you teach your son's son.
— *The Talmud*

As we look at our own life history and begin to understand how we reached this point, we have to examine what was passed on to us by our parents and then realize that they were doing the best they could with what they had been given. We talk about the chain of transmission through generations who had problems with addictions and codependency. Many of us know that we want to break that chain so that our children don't inherit the negative patterns.

How do we break the chain of generation after generation of addiction and abuse? We become the best father we know how to be. We develop genuine relationships with our children, letting them truly know us; we tell them about our lives and listen to them talk about their lives. It isn't all about discipline; it's about having a bond and being honest in telling our children that we love and care for them. Certainly, setting limits and being consistent are important tenets, but the most important thing a father can give his child is letting his child know him.

Today, I will be engaged with my child
in a genuine and open relationship.

*In prayer it is better to have a heart without
words than words without a heart.*
— John Bunyan

Prayer starts with openness in our heart and with self-honesty. We don't sit down to ask special favors from God to achieve our ego's rewards. We quiet our mind. For a brief time, we release all the particular details, the worries and tasks that have been rushing in on us. In this quiet space, we consciously focus our attention on our relationship with our Higher Power. This is a very private, personal relationship, known intimately only by us. Even our search for this relationship, even the question "Where are you, God?" is a prayer.

This healing journey has two aspects. One aspect is fellowship with others, the healing of our separation from our fellow men. The other aspect is a deeply private relationship with our Higher Power. When we have spent some quiet time in prayer, echoes of that prayer stay with us in the back of our mind, no matter how busy and focused we become on our daily tasks.

*Today, I open my heart with honesty
to my Higher Power.*

To age with dignity and with courage
cuts close to what it is to be a man.
— *Roger Kahn*

The healing journey requires courage. We are walking a path that is somewhat off the mainstream. We seek to become better men, better friends, better intimate partners, and better fathers. We seek to grow out of our self-centeredness to be more generous and caring. It takes courage to give up the pursuit of greater and greater control, to give up the empty pursuit of happiness through more material possessions. Courage comes forward when we refuse to use our old escapes and accept our problems so we can deal with them.

Nothing is so bad that it can't be talked about. When we choose a trustworthy friend to tell our truth to, we see our situation from new angles. We can then have a dialogue with our friend and within ourselves that leads to a new outlook and new solutions. This kind of connection with other men creates new integrity within ourselves and gives us genuine dignity.

Today, I will continue to have courage
on my journey of healing.

· APRIL 7 ·

*Be not forgetful to entertain strangers:
for thereby some have entertained angels
unaware.*

— Hebrews 13:2

Recovery is a very democratic thing. No matter how far down a man has fallen, no matter how bad his life choices have been or how much he has given up for his addiction and codependency, he deserves our basic human respect. We all are created in the image of God. There is something of God within everyone.

When we go to our meetings, we meet many kinds of people. Some of them we have more in common with than others. Some of them we will feel closer to than others. But we are all creatures of the universe, and we are all equally loved by God. We may feel critical of someone's behavior, but ultimately we are called to respect everyone as fellow human beings seeking a path through life.

*Today, I accept the love of God and pledge
to show respect to everyone I meet.*

To "be" means to be related.
—Alfred Korzybski

In our using and codependent days, loneliness was ever-present. We could be with a crowd, but we felt alienated and alone. Many of us grew up in families where no one really knew how to feel close. We often longed for a closer connection with our fathers. As adult men, we learned to be self-sufficient, and we thought it was always superior to be able to do something without help. If we got help to accomplish something, it was somehow not quite as good as if we did it alone.

Now we are part of a fellowship with other men and women who know what it's like to be where we have been; they are on the same journey. We may have very different lives in some ways, but we have our common goal: to become better people. The true basis for our humanity, the real fulfillment of our potential, is in relationship with others. We no longer have to be locked in our isolated world. Through our friendships and our spiritual path, we are free to be ourselves.

Today, I am grateful for my friends.

*The coming to consciousness is not a discovery
of some new thing; it is a long and painful return
to that which has always been.*

— Helen Luke

When a few guys in Ohio first developed the Twelve Steps of Alcoholics Anonymous, they didn't just sit down to devise a way to help alcoholics. The Steps were born out of the pain and desperation of men in the grips of a disease that seemed hopeless and terminal. By trial and error, they wrestled with this grip of addiction, slowly uncovering an approach that was helping them to stay sober. It was only after awakening in their new life of sobriety that they started to define and write down the steps they had taken.

In some ways, to reach our awakening we all must pass through the same process of pain and challenge that those men in Ohio did. No life is free of pain. The best of us take our pain and seek to use it as a learning tool. We ask how we can make something positive out of our distress. We take stock of where we are and accept it as our starting point for moving forward. When we awaken to consciousness through the Twelve Steps, it is a unique and personal story, and yet it is a universal human story.

Today, I give thanks for my growing consciousness.

The problem is this: skills learned in danger
require the presence of danger to be effective.
— Wayne Muller

Many of us had stressful childhoods. Some of us lived in chaotic households. Some of us were badly treated by the people we relied on to take care of us. Life often felt dangerous, but we developed skills to deal with the chaos. Some of us learned to keep things to ourselves, some of us learned to please those around us, and some of us learned to avoid all confrontation or disagreement.

These childhood skills, learned through hard lessons in the presence of danger, may have become fixed in our immature minds. But in our adult lives, those dangers may no longer be present. No one is beating us up anymore, but we are still flinching. The door is open for us to walk out, but we now must learn the skills of living in a safer world. We can take small steps by saying how we feel, by opening our hearts to trusted friends, and by asking for what we would like and being generous with others. These skills can be learned. As we gain this knowledge, we have more and more rewarding lives.

Today, I will take some risks that are my privilege
as an adult, even if they seem risky.

Where there is fear, we lose the way of our spirit.
— *Mahatma Gandhi*

We don't like to admit that we are afraid. But when we won't admit the feeling, we can't deal with it. By denying our fears, we don't get stronger, we weaken ourselves. Denying fear doesn't get rid of problems, it only reinforces them. In the end, if we don't handle fear well, it rules us.

Fear is a universal human emotion, and we cannot eradicate it. We must learn how to handle the hot coals of fear. When we learn how, they don't have to be destructive. Handling fear begins with self-knowledge. We first learn that the unsettling feeling we have may be fear. Our desire to run away, or the tight knot in our gut, may be fear. That admission to ourselves can be followed by talking about it to a friend or a sponsor. Sometimes just speaking the fear out loud to someone we trust is enough to put it back in perspective. We have handled it.

*Today, I will notice my feelings and respond
to feelings of fear in constructive ways.*

Between stimulus and response,
man has the freedom to choose.
— *Stephen R. Covey*

Ancient wise men first identified that crucial gap in time between the moment we first sense something and the response we give. They taught meditation principles focusing on this distinction and spent hours in contemplation that led to deep inner peace and serenity. Most of us, in our busy lives, do not devote hours and days to that focus, but we can learn to practice the crucial wisdom of chosen response instead of instant reflex.

Reactivity is like a knee-jerk response. It comes from a primitive part of our brains. If we haven't learned of that brief gap between the stimulus and our response, then we don't even know we have a choice. We might say, "I couldn't help it. If he hadn't done that, I wouldn't have done what I did." At that point, we are still immature and weak. When we gain awareness of this tiny bit of time to choose the best response, we step from immaturity into the strength of a grown man.

Today, I will become more aware of that moment
of choice between a stimulus and my response.

How many cares one loses when one decides
not to be something, but to be someone.
— Coco Chanel

Why are we working so hard? What are we striving
toward? Do we want to achieve some important accomplishment, or do we want to be someone we respect?
Naturally we don't have just one aim. We have many
goals and hopes, but what are the most important ones?

When we focus on becoming the best kind of person
we know how to be, we leave behind all our anxieties
about how well we can perform. We still need to accomplish tasks and do our work, but the important thing now
is the kind of person we are while we are doing them.
Are we honest? Are we considerate of others? Is our
heart open to the world? Do we take responsibility
for our actions? When we fulfill the personal qualities
that we admire, we can allow ourselves some slack for
mistakes and imperfection in our achievements.

Today, I am grateful that I am
becoming someone I respect.

God should be sought, but we cannot find God.
We can only be found by God.

— *Henri Nouwen*

As we develop spiritually, we get to know in our own lives the mysteries and paradoxes that great thinkers have written about. True spiritual development is an ever-deepening lesson in powerlessness and letting go. We seek God, but our seeking is really only our preparation to receive God. We don't make the willful decision to find God. We only decide to be open and to stop standing in the way of God's purposes in our lives.

When a man falls asleep, sleep doesn't come when he works at it. It comes only when, in his mind, he stops working at anything. He decides to go to bed and fall asleep, but then he simply lies back and allows it to happen. If, in his mind, he is still busy working, he will not sleep. Something like that is true in all matters of letting go. We must learn how to stop getting in the way of spiritual influences in our lives, and our only power is to become entirely ready to receive them.

Today, I will let go of my self-centered willfulness
and be open to the greater powers at work.

Spring is when you feel like whistling
even with a shoe full of slush.
— *Doug Larson*

Life is never just one thing. It is quite possible to feel optimistic and happy even when some things are not right with us. An optimistic outlook gives us energy to handle the harder challenges we have to deal with. Research shows that people who have a positive attitude have a stronger immune system, are healthier, live longer, and are even more likely to recover from serious illness.

To believe in hopeful outcomes is largely a matter of choice. Many of us have experienced big disappointments and defeats in life. But having come this far, we can look back and see that somehow we had the capacity to deal with it. The Second Step guides us to believe in hopeful possibilities. We can't say that things will always turn out just the way we hope, but that we can cope with whatever happens.

Today, I choose to believe that a Power
greater than myself can help me deal with life,
and I have reason to be optimistic.

Anger is a great energizer if you don't get stuck in it.
— *Lavonne Stewart*

Many of us have to face up to our anger and the negative ways we have handled it. For most men, the real problem is not anger itself, but how we express it. Some of us never express it; others of us get abusive when we express it. Either way calls for more growth. Often, people confuse anger with abuse. They may say, "I just have to express my feelings, and when I'm angry, I have to let it out." Other people say, "Anger is so hurtful. I will avoid it at all costs."

Healing requires that we look to see the sources of our anger, how we have expressed it or failed to, and then learn how to say our feelings honestly and with respect. When we see what we are actually angry about, it gives us energy, it motivates us. It's a life force. There is no rule that we have to show our anger in destructive ways. We can be flat-out angry at someone we love and still maintain the respect we hold for that person. It is possible to learn to look at a friend and say, "I feel angry about this, and I'm here to tell you about it because I care about our friendship."

Today, I will accept my angry feelings as a source of life energy, and I will find honest, respectful ways to show them.

Discipline is remembering what you want.
— David Campbell

Not everyone chooses recovery easily. We were attached to our addictions and codependency, even if we didn't want their consequences. They were not only our masters; we were also loyal to them. They gave us comfort, pleasure, and a high that nothing else could match. So where did we find motivation to change?

Somewhere within our souls we longed for something of greater quality. We didn't want to sacrifice our future for the fleeting pleasures or false escapes. We saw that our actions were ruining our own lives and the lives of our loved ones. We always thought we would change someday, and even while our lives were careening out of control, we promised ourselves to change tomorrow or sometime in the future. It was our greater vision, our longing for a better life, that led us to try the Twelve Step recovery program. Out of wanting something better we found the motivation to enter recovery.

Today, I know that deep in my soul
lies a desire to be a good man.

Thought is action in rehearsal.
— *Sigmund Freud*

We sometimes indulge ourselves in fantasies and images of things we would like to do, or in euphoric recall of what we did in the past. Thoughts are powerful forces, and the ways we use them will shape our development. An Olympic diver creates vivid images of the perfect dive in his mind as part of his training because his thoughts help him perform at the crucial moment. Even in recovery, we are sometimes tempted to revisit former ecstatic moments from our using days, or to dream about a return to using but with better control the next time. We need to keep in mind that these thoughts serve as rehearsals for later action. They only weaken our recovery.

What kind of thoughts shall we cultivate in our minds? We can picture ourselves feeling relaxed and peaceful, having the craving lifted from us. We can picture ourselves maintaining a serene detachment while confronted with crisis. We can picture a situation with a loved one in which we say what we need to say and feel good about staying true to ourselves. This is the way to use our minds to rehearse for future action.

*Today, I will hold an image of myself
feeling relaxed and safe, even in the
midst of confusion around me.*

When one door closes another door opens;
but we often look so long and so regretfully
upon the closed door that we do not see the
ones which open for us.
— *Alexander Graham Bell*

Change is a basic fact of life, and with every change comes a loss. Even winning the lottery entails the loss of our life before the big win. During some periods of our life, we feel we are stuck and nothing changes, or we feel trapped in a situation we would love to change. Other times a change occurs that we would never choose, and we have to find a way to continue living with the new reality.

Coping with the closing and opening of doors is a fundamental spiritual matter. We are pilgrims on a journey and much of what happens along our way is beyond our control. Today will bring some things that we did not expect, and with the changes will be new possibilities that we did not expect. So we hold the spiritual attitude that while we cannot control what happens, we can choose how we will respond.

Today, I pray for the spiritual vision
to see the doors that open for me.

My dear child, you must believe in God
in spite of what the clergy tell you.
— *Benjamin Jowett*

We come to the Twelve Step program of recovery from many different backgrounds. Some of us already have a very solid spiritual base to call on. Some of us have a blank, undeveloped sense of spirituality and an open mind. Some of us had negative or even abusive experiences with organized religion, so we turned away from all ideas of spirituality. Now we are following a path that asks us to turn our lives and will over to God, and our past experience may tell us to say no to such a proposition.

Still, we want to recover, and our previous methods didn't work, so now we are willing to have an open mind about "the God thing." Maybe we can learn something we never understood before. The concept of God was controversial even among the people who first developed this path. They all knew that spiritual reliance was crucial to recovery, but they didn't all believe in God in the same way. So they landed on the phrase, "God *as we understood Him*." Wisely, they made the program's spirituality a very big tent, and there is room for every individual's beliefs.

Today, I am grateful for the spirituality
that this program has nurtured within me.

Love at first sight is easy to understand. It's when two people have been looking at each other for years that it becomes a miracle.

— Sam Levenson

True intimacy introduces us to ourselves. A loving relationship is the greatest therapy. When we first fall in love, we are filled with optimism. We cling to all the best qualities of the person we fall in love with, and we look past those things we don't like. But an intimate partnership takes us further than we've been before.

Most of us fall in love and soon find ourselves in over our heads. We haven't had experience in sustaining openness and vulnerability. We may gradually begin to feel too exposed. The relationship tests our ability to trust someone who has this much access to our inner self. We become cranky or overly sensitive. We may test our partner's love by asking, "If you love me, will you do such and such?" We begin to try to control our partner so we don't feel so vulnerable. All these temptations are holdover behaviors from our less mature selves. So we must reach for our more mature selves and trust that we can survive being so vulnerable.

Today, I will turn to my Higher Power for guidance in going forward in trust while being vulnerable.

I go to nature to be soothed and healed,
and to have my senses put in order.
— *John Burroughs*

In the Twelve Steps, we see the term *God* several times. But from the program's beginning, there have been atheists and agnostics using and valuing the Steps as their guide for life. Many men do not relate to a personal God. They do, however, experience the meaning and spirit of their group and the restoring powers of nature. That is why the founders of Alcoholics Anonymous included the phrase "God *as we understood Him.*"

Whether a personal God is real to us or not, nature is there for us as a healing and refreshing source. We don't have to go on a major trip to the mountains or fishing in the wilderness to find this source. We find it in the sky, the clouds, and the magical moon; we find it in the intricate structure of a leaf, a massive tree in the park, or a wild bird on a window ledge. There is no more clear evidence of the generous gifts that come unbidden than in nature. And we can rest in the Power greater than ourselves shown in creation and the forces of nature.

Today, I will be soothed and healed
by nature all around.

We must find some spiritual basis
for living, else we die.
— Bill Wilson

When one of the founders of Alcoholics Anonymous wrote these words, he was speaking from the perspective of a recovering man. He knew that his addiction would kill him if he didn't base his life on a spiritual footing. There is also such a thing as being spiritually dead while our physical bodies are still alive. Whether we are recovering from addiction or codependency, or walking some other healing path, our life force is rooted in our spiritual connection.

Just as an addiction grows and progresses through the span of our lives, so too, if we are consciously attentive, our spiritual development continues through the years of our lives. We grow stronger, become more accepting of ourselves and others, and feel more connected to the people and the world we live in.

Today, conscious contact with my
creator keeps me alive.

*You see the one that I am, not the one
that I was. But the one that I was is
also still part of myself.*

—Jean Améry

Our stories are central to our recovery. We tell them because they remind us where we came from. We live in the present moment, but our history is part of our identity. It isn't the total of our identity, but it informs our healing. It's the mine where we dig for the nuggets of wisdom for living today, and it gives us the drive and encouragement to continue our progress. We don't tell our stories to wallow in the shame and guilt we felt or to gain sympathy for our suffering. And we don't tell them to revel in the euphoria of the highs we experienced.

In telling our stories, others get to know us better because our history is part of our very selves. In that process, we cannot help but listen to ourselves speak the truth, and we thereby put together the puzzle pieces of our selves. Taking the risk of saying where we came from provides the rewards of feeling accepted by others.

*I am grateful for telling my story and knowing
that I am more than the man I once was.*

*Listen to your body. Do not be
a blind and deaf tenant.*
— Dr. George Sheehan

We were taught that masculinity means ignoring pain, disregarding the sensations that arise within our bodies. A warrior in battle needs to do that to save his life. When a man can ignore his pain because of a more pressing goal, he has a valuable skill. But we aren't living in a battle zone every day. And a wise man uses his skills selectively. When we are walking down an open sidewalk on a sunny, warm day, we use different skills than when walking on ice.

Part of our recovery requires that we grow beyond some of the stereotypes of what a man is. A one-trick pony can't adapt to a new show. When we are in the safety of an intimate relationship, we need to know what we feel and express it. We need the skills to pay attention to our internal messages, because they are also guides.

*Today, I will have the wisdom to listen
to the messages of my body and my heart.*

Although the world is full of suffering,
it is full also of the overcoming of it.
— *Helen Keller*

We are born into a life with both pain and joy. That mix is inevitable, no matter what our status in life. If today's combination seems more filled with difficulty or challenge, it also contains the possibilities for coping with it. We can take some steps today that will move us toward overcoming our challenges. We must avoid feeling defeated if we cannot totally fix our problems all at once. And most certainly, there are unseen forces at work, forces that continually bring change. Let us accept that life always changes. Never can we place a clamp on some perfect day and hold ourselves there permanently. So we ride the ups and downs, we meet our pain and suffering, and we overcome it.

Today, as I face difficulty and rise to its challenges,
I will have an attitude of acceptance.

Dream as if you'll live forever.
Live as if you'll die today.
                    — *James Dean*

To live as if we will die tomorrow means to feel very alive right now. It means to be spiritually alert in the present moment with an open heart and full awareness of our experience. To dream as if we will live forever means we hold a vision and a sense of values that act as a compass on our path, directing our daily choices. We know how it felt to be lost or trapped and already half dead. That was before our rebirth in recovery. One of life's paradoxes is that when we accept our ultimate powerlessness of death, we are freed to live life at its fullest. This is not the path that most adults follow. It is easy to lapse into a less alive, less spiritually alert style. But on our healing journey, we cannot afford that.

Today, I am grateful for this day
and this moment of life.

I don't want everyone to like me; I should
think less of myself if some people did.
                                        — *Henry James*

When we don't know ourselves very well, we may be
desperate to have everyone like us. Sometimes we even
notice more intently that one person who doesn't seem
to like us than the many who do. We are looking outward
to verify that we are okay. Of course, it feels good to
have someone else like and respect us. Until we begin to
know and accept ourselves, we have an unquenchable,
unselective thirst for more applause from others. In that
condition, the search for others' approval drives us like
the need for survival.

It is amazing how our sense of ourselves grows as we
live in the Twelve Step program. We get to know ourselves by working the Steps, and we develop into the
kind of men we respect. Now, having others like us is no
longer a survival need. It is a wonderful benefit of being
part of the human community.

Today, I am grateful for the true
friendships that I have in my life.

If you are going through hell, keep going.
— *Winston Churchill*

Some days, some weeks, even some years seem like hell. We give our best to life and still it continues to be hard. A future with some measure of pain and problems is inevitable from the very day of our birth. That may seem like a bleak reality, and it is what we may call hell. But it is also the very thing that shapes our learning and development into good men.

These times of challenge and heartache call us to keep going. They are a source of spiritual lessons for us. If today finds us in the midst of such difficulty, we can know that we are never alone. Our Higher Power is always with us. We can talk to a friend and reveal what is happening in our life. And we can also know that, as bad as any time might be, life is always a mixture that includes some blessings and something to be grateful for.

Today, I will keep going forward.

*An expert is a man who has made all the mistakes
that can be made in a narrow field.*

— Niels Bohr

At the time they happen, mistakes are always deeply
regrettable. No one ever sets out to make a mistake. But
fortunately, we are not seeking perfection. We weren't
born fully clothed with an instruction book on how to
live. We don't learn anything new from doing the things
we already have down pat. Mistakes are how we learn,
and some of those lessons are painful indeed. A man who
is afraid to risk a mistake shields himself from growing.

So we take risks, knowing we will make mistakes.
There is no shame in a mistake that we learn from. It
is said that the truly wise man keeps his beginner's attitude and is always open to learning. Many of us can say
that if mistakes create an expert, then we must be well
qualified already. And in fact, for those of us who have
learned from them, we truly are smarter and stronger
for the experience. The key is first to discard the notion
of perfectionism, then to take the reasonable risks that
may lead to mistakes, and finally to learn the lessons
contained in them.

*Today, I am grateful for my life experience, and I will
continue to take reasonable risks and grow.*

MAY

Our Lord has written the promise of
resurrection, not in books alone but
in every leaf of springtime.
— Martin Luther

Springtime is a perfect metaphor for renewed life, recovery, and resurrection. All around us we see the buds of leaves and flowers bursting forth in celebration. Just like nature, we, too, experience our personal springtime of renewal. Our personal anniversaries are worthy of celebration, whether it be one day, one month, or many years of recovery.

Some people are shy about celebrating their days and years of recovery. Maybe they feel unworthy, or they don't want to draw attention to themselves. But the true spirit of celebration is humility. It's not because we have worked so hard that we deserve it; it's that we have been given the gift promised in the Twelve Steps. Because we submit to the grace of God, we celebrate the gift we have received.

Today, I see the symbols of renewed life
within me and all around.

If you come to a fork in the road, take it.
— *Yogi Berra*

The humor in this quotation points to some deeper wisdom. The fact is, we all come to forks in the road of life, and we have to choose which way to go. Sometimes we cannot see a clear best choice. Sometimes we know what the best choice would be, but we cannot face the losses or the pain it would entail. Many of us have stopped at the fork in the road and just sat there for a long, long time, refusing to take either way.

The healthy, creative, constructive life requires some risk-taking. Even when we are not sure which is the best way to go, it may be better to try one of them than to just stay stuck. Certainly, it is wise to stop, consider our choices, and not be too hasty or impulsive. But after we think and weigh the options, making a choice will lead to new information, which will then influence our next choices. That is how we follow a creative and lively path for ourselves.

Today, I will remember that
some risk-taking is healthy.

*When you have got an elephant by the
hind leg, and he is trying to run away,
it's best to let him run.*
                                — *Abraham Lincoln*

We know what it feels like to have an elephant by the
hind leg when he wants to run. We have held on to our
addictive and codependent ways, thinking we were in
control and refusing to face the reality that we were
about to get trampled. Now we can be grateful for the
guidance of Step One. When we could admit we were
not in control, that changed everything.

Some of us knew we were out of control but didn't
know where to go from there. We were living in despair,
but with no place to turn. Steps One and Two pointed
the way to a spiritual release. We were told that if we "let
the elephant go," we could get help from a Higher Power.
This new way of thinking gave us a whole different take
on our life. We can let go, and we will survive.

*Today, I am grateful for the
life-changing option of letting go.*

Working so hard for the rewards we want,
we miss the gifts, already present, that God
wants to give us.

— *Anonymous*

We cannot win many of the good things in life; we can
only receive them. It is like falling asleep. No one can
will himself to sleep. If we could, there would be no
such thing as a sleepless night. The harder we try, the
more awake we become. We can only *allow* ourselves to
fall asleep. We cannot create a sunny day or a beautiful
sight in nature, but we can block them from our awareness. We cannot fall in love by force of will, but we can
prevent it from happening by our willfulness or busy
habits. Our raging appetites and anxious state of mind
can drive us willy-nilly in search of satisfaction—while
more profound gifts are already in our hands.

Many valuable gifts are available only if we stay open
to receive them. A wise man grows past our society's
mainstream idea that anything worth having requires
hard work. The ultimate truth is that God's grace provides what we need. Our work is in learning how to let
go and be receptive.

Today, I will open myself to the
gifts already in my hands.

Don't brood on what's past,
but never forget it either.
— *Thomas H. Raddall*

When we make big changes in our lives for the better, as we have all done, we naturally grieve the time we lost by not learning our lessons sooner. There's no way to avoid that grief, but there's no point in dwelling on it. Some of us get hooked by feelings of regret. We brood over the ways we let others down, and we wish we could relive certain events and do better with them this time. It is important for us all to release the past—let it go. Our life is now. If we spend our conscious moments living in the past and regretting our mistakes, we never get on with living a good life in the present. A truly humble man accepts the forgiveness of others and the forgiveness of his Higher Power. He accepts the universal truth that we are all broken in some ways, and our self-acceptance isn't based on what we did or didn't do in the past, but on how we live today.

Today, I look back at where I have come
from and feel grateful for a new life.

Memory is the diary we all carry about with us.
— *Oscar Wilde*

Our memories create the substance of our identity. People who lose their memory lose any sense of who they are. Some of us have memories of painful events in our childhood, or of traumas that changed our image of ourselves. Those of us who were abused by parents have to learn in adulthood to fill those gaps by becoming good parents to ourselves. Some of us have become trapped at a younger stage of development by painful memories. Now, it is essential to our healing that we not perpetuate our own abuse.

We have to learn to include ourselves in the human family. No matter what we experienced, no matter what we feel, it is all part of what it means to be human. We can heal our memories, not by changing them, but by making peace with them so we are free to live in the present. A man can imagine the little boy he once was— and imagine taking that youngster on his lap and promising him that he will take care of him and keep him safe.

Today, I will be a good parent to myself
and treat myself with love and respect.

> *[Everyone] "writes" in a way; that is, each person has a "story"—a personal narrative—which is constantly being replayed, revised, taken apart and put together again.*
>
> — *Margaret Atwood*

Central to our healing and recovery are telling our story and hearing the stories others have to tell. Something changes when we first speak out loud to another person to tell what we were like, what we have experienced, and what we feel now. Most people feel great relief when they say what they have on their minds. Often we don't fully know what we feel or think until we put it into words. The telling of it to an attentive listener bridges the gap between us.

Putting our stories into words gives them a form they didn't have before and gives us handles to begin to deal with our experience. When we tell the story of our pain, our mistakes, and our triumphs, the words are the symbols that allow us to let go and move on.

Today, I will talk to someone about my experience, describing either a small feeling or a big one.

Some things have to be believed to be seen.
— *Ralph Hodgson*

Under the guidance of this recovery program we "came to believe that a Power greater than ourselves could restore us to sanity." Coming to believe something is a process. It might begin by borrowing someone else's faith, trying it on as we might try on a shirt. We don't start with a firm conviction. We don't grow instantly from no faith to absolute faith. It might begin by seeing that forces are at work beyond our control, easing our terrible cravings or supporting us through the worst times.

Sometimes faith develops very slowly, like the first sprout of an acorn in the spring. At our meetings, we encounter men who are like mighty oaks, but years ago, they were just beginning to send up tender sprouts. This process certainly takes us beyond what we can explain with rational description. We don't have to understand it.

*Today, I am grateful for the faith that allows
me to see what I could not otherwise see.*

God as the ultimate mystery
of being is beyond thinking.
— Joseph Campbell

The child's profound question "Where did I come from?"
never really gets answered as long as we live. We learn
to settle for things that point to an answer, for bits of
evidence of partial answers. Holy scriptures tell us what
wise people said over the millennia. But in the end, our
thinking isn't big enough to encompass or understand
the ultimate mystery.

Yet it seems to be in the nature of our human race to
think in spiritual terms and to embrace mystery. We are
in awe when we see the vastness of the ocean, when we
gaze across the vista from a mountainside, or when we
look through a microscope at the inner workings of a
cell. This feeling of awe and beauty, and the mystery it
evokes, is the spiritual impulse. The mystery brought us
here, and when we follow it, we can learn to trust it. It
gives us our birthright to be here, and it will care for us.

Today, I am in the care of God, and I will
accept the comfort of trusting God.

*One of the oldest human needs is having
someone to wonder where you are when
you don't come home at night.*
— Margaret Mead

Many of us grew up with a loving mother who gave us life and cared for our needs. Others among us had mothers who were missing from our lives, either physically or emotionally. Perhaps no word in any language carries more weight or more feelings than the word *mother*. It carries images of comfort, undying love, first intimacy, and complete acceptance. Few mothers ever totally fulfill those images.

As we become adults, we have a more realistic understanding of our relationship with our mother. She was a real human being, not a stereotype, and not perfect. We longed for her approval and her love, as all children do. We had angry feelings toward her sometimes, and guilt about the ways we hurt her. It is our adult task to make peace with her, living or dead, to forgive her for what we did not get and for how we were hurt, and to accept forgiveness for our mistakes. Only after we have made that peace are we truly emancipated adults and free to love others fully.

Today, I seek peace with my mother.

It is only by risking our persons from
one hour to another that we live at all.
— William James

We all know men who seem to be empty bodies, walking through life. These are the guys who never talk about anything personal and never let anyone get to know them. Many of them love to complain about their job, their spouse or partner, their boss, the government, or anything outside themselves. These guys will talk about sports or the weather but never about real events or personal experiences. Many of us have been these men.

When we wake up to a real life, we become present; we are alive to our experiences, our sensations, and our feelings. This requires that we drop the shield of deadness and become personal. It involves risk and makes life incredibly interesting.

Today, I will take the risk to be present
to my life in every minute, every hour.

*Just as we took refuge in being special, we can learn
to take refuge in being ordinary, not being in charge,
not being the center of the universe.*

— *Wayne Muller*

In our addictive and codependent minds, we were prone
to feeling special. We felt grandiose about our power to
fix others, or about our power to walk on the edge of
danger and not get hurt. We thought we could handle
things that most people couldn't. Some of us felt especially bad and shameful, more shameful than everyone
else. We thought recovery was fine for others, but it
wasn't what we needed, or it wasn't going to work for us.

True self-esteem is not based on feeling special or
better than others. A large ingredient of true self-esteem
is self-respecting humility. We are all much more alike
than we are different, and we are connected to each
other on the basic levels of life and death, pain and joy,
and the need to give and receive love. When we make
friends with other men and really let them know us, we
feel our common humanity and a strong sense of self-
acceptance and self-esteem.

*Today, I will notice my connection with all others,
the people I like and the ones I dislike, the people
I know and the people who are strangers.*

You can't control the wind, but you can
adjust your sails.
— *Fortune cookie message*

Sailing is both peaceful and adventurous. Imagine being on a sailboat, working the sails to use the wind for quiet, controlled movement or for exciting speed as you skim across the water. It's a skill that improves with experience. You learn to work with the wind and apply it to your advantage. Anyone who tries to sail his boat willfully, contrary to the conditions of the wind, gets nowhere.

A well-lived life also draws on experience, and we continue to learn as long as we live. Our male role models told us that masculinity meant conquering our surroundings, and many of us instinctively saw competition and confrontation as a matter of personal honor. We believed that, as men, our self-esteem was tied to subduing any obstacle before us. But those were a boy's ideas about what a man is like.

As we grow wiser and genuinely stronger, we set our sails to work with the wind. We can neither stop the wind nor make it blow.

Today, I will watch the winds in my life
and work with them to live better.

· MAY 14 ·

*It's not so much that we're afraid of change or
so in love with the old ways, but it's that place
in between that we fear. . . . It's Linus when his
blanket is in the dryer. There's nothing to hold
on to.*

— *Marilyn Ferguson*

The big change for us is moving beyond our addiction
and codependency. Many of us didn't feel very attached
to our addiction, but we didn't know what to do without it. We didn't feel "normal" when we weren't using,
and it didn't seem right to stop taking charge of others'
problems. It was hard to imagine what else to do with
our time, and hard to build another way of living.

In many other smaller ways, we are called on to let go
of what is familiar and move into what is not yet known.
This is an uncomfortable but very creative space. We
know our growth was stopped by our old ways. Now,
with the courage to tolerate the discomfort, we can leave
our less mature selves behind and grow to become better
men.

*Today, I will tolerate feeling awkward and
uncomfortable while I keep growing.*

There is no smaller package in the world than
that of a person all wrapped up in himself.
— William Sloane Coffin

In self-centeredness, we are trapped within the confines of our own skin. It is a self-indulgence that stifles and chokes our emotional development by continuously turning us back into our own limitations, pain, and fears. The grandiose feeling of superiority is not the only way that self-centeredness grabs and holds us; feelings of shame and self-pity can also trap us. To liberate ourselves from these traps, we first get acquainted with them and name the feelings, which gives us some power over them. Next, we get outside ourselves by reaching out to help someone else who is genuinely in need.

When we have a cause or a purpose greater than our own selfish goals, we escape the boundaries of our self. That's the spiritual move toward participating in the larger whole.

Today, I will help someone simply out of generosity,
or I will help with a cause that's greater than myself.

Gossip needn't be false to be evil—there's a lot of truth that shouldn't be passed around.
— Frank A. Clark

To be a friend is a trust placed in us. Naturally, as we get to know someone better, and we grow closer over time, he lets us into his more private and personal world, and he does that in a spirit of trust. In a sense, he is saying we may come past the fence that keeps most people out because he trusts us. Maybe he even lets us know some guarded secrets about his life. We need to be sure that we live up to the trust placed in us. Our self-respect and our character are at stake: how loyally do we honor that trust?

When we attend our meetings, we hear many things that are spoken in trust. Hearing someone's story is a privilege and an honor, and with that comes our duty to honor and protect the privacy of our fellow members. When someone takes us into his privacy, it becomes our job to protect it. If we fail to keep his trust, it reflects on us as not worthy of the honor.

Today, I am grateful for the chance to know other men and women so well that they share their private lives with me. I honor that trust by protecting their privacy.

We don't pay our sponsors for their time. Instead, we pay it forward. We turn around and help the next person. That's how the whole thing works.
— *Michael Graubart*

We all stand on the shoulders of those who have been our teachers, and on the shoulders of those who taught our teachers. When we pick a sponsor for our recovery, we look for someone we admire and trust, someone who has demonstrated success in his recovery.

Perhaps we feel we have a long way to go and a lot to learn. Perhaps we are struck by the big job we have ahead. But all we need to do is make progress. And we don't have to reinvent the wheel. When we learn from our sponsor and from other people in our recovery community who are making progress, we get to stand on their shoulders. They let us see much more than we could see alone.

Today, I am grateful for all the benefits of having a good sponsor.

When you aim for perfection you
discover it's a moving target.
— George Fisher

In our desire for control, we seek the ultimate control of perfection. We try to relieve our anxieties and self-doubts by achieving it, but in fact we perpetuate our unease by seeking what cannot be attained. Some of us say, "I'm not a perfectionist because I am far from perfect," only proving that we are always measuring ourselves with that yardstick.

The way to resolve this dilemma is to get a different yardstick. Instead of measuring how far we are from perfect, we could measure whether we are learning anything new. Or we can ask ourselves if we have continued to get back on the path when we veer off course. Knowing we will make mistakes, we can ask ourselves if we take responsibility for them. Knowing some things will go wrong, no matter how well we plan, we can include in our plans a vision to accept mistakes as part of the package.

Today, I will try to learn from whatever happens,
and when something goes wrong, I will accept it
and deal with it.

*How we spend our days is, of course,
how we spend our lives.*
— Annie Dillard

Today *is* our life. Even though we are drawn to live in the past or have fears and hopes for the future, we only exist in the present. This moment is all we have, and it is enough. There is no need to center our thoughts on how things will turn out in the future because we are alive right now, and this is our life. Our memories exist only in our minds; they enrich the present, but we have no opportunity to relive them.

As we live in this moment and center our awareness in this moment, we have a sense that we can deal with it. Feeling overwhelmed comes from trying to take too big of a bite of time. It's more than anyone can swallow. In this moment, as we sit in our place, we have sensations of sight and sound and touch. We can deal with this moment and that is all we need to do . . . ever. Centered in this very time and this very place, we regain our peace of mind and our ability to live well.

Today is all I need, for today is my life.

When you lose, do not lose the lesson.
— *H. Jackson Brown Jr.*

The only mistakes we are doomed to repeat are the ones we fail to learn from. Life is a matter of approximating our goals, seldom a matter of hitting the bullseye. We take risks, sometimes we fail to understand what we are dealing with, and sometimes we just indulge ourselves in what we want regardless of what is good for us. So, in some ways, we are constantly remeasuring the difference between what we aimed for and what we actually achieved.

If we only mourn the loss or berate ourselves for missing the target and never use it to learn, we have truly lost something important. It is when we call on our inner resources and learn the lesson that we get better and stronger. Learning is the most important part of our life journey.

Today, I will look for the lessons in my mistakes and let go of defeatist attitudes.

*A man does not seek to see himself in running
water, but in still water. For only what is itself
still can impart stillness to others.*

— *Zhuang Zhou*

Our own reactivity has often escalated a problem rather
than helped to resolve it. But we can learn to be less
reactive. All of us have a range of responses. At our worst
we may lash out in abusive anger. At our best we try to
be tolerant and understanding. When we are exhausted
or depleted in other ways, we are more prone to react
from our worst self. And our harsh reaction only makes
a crisis worse.

We can change our pattern of reactivity and give our
best response by developing an inner calm. Then we
always have access to our better self, and we are less
prone to take things personally. That doesn't mean we
are always placid or passive, because sometimes our best
self needs to rise up and say *no!* When we are calm, we
can respond most effectively, either with open tolerance
or with a "no" if it is called for.

*Today, I will maintain an inner calm
as I deal with the issues that arise.*

Whoever thinks that marriage is a fifty-fifty
proposition doesn't know the half of it.
— *Franklin P. Jones*

Naturally, we expect our intimate partnerships to be built on equality and mutuality. Sometimes we get so focused on the role our partner is playing that we lose focus on our own. A good intimate partnership works when we stay focused on being a worthy partner and stop keeping score.

We nourish our intimate relationship by being respectful, kind, and generous, whether or not we feel our partner is doing the same. That doesn't mean that we never talk about what we want or hope for from our partner. It simply means that our loving attitude isn't contingent on whether we get what we want. We know what a good partner is like, and when we provide that, it enhances the whole relationship and inspires our partner to respect us and respond in kind.

Today, I will be the best partner I know
how to be, regardless of what I receive.

*Seeing first one's own defects and shortcomings
is Humility; the fruit of that vision is Tolerance.*
— *Ernest Kurtz and Katherine Ketcham*

The word *humble* has its roots in the Latin word for earth, *humus*. That doesn't mean that if I am humble I feel like dirt. It means that the earth is truly my mother. My flesh and bones, like all living creatures, are made of earth— nothing more and nothing less.

When I gain humility, I have myself in perspective. I like myself and I see how much I have in common with all my fellow human beings. This is truly a gift that I receive as part of living a spiritual life. It means I have acceptance and peace of mind. I don't have to constantly compete. I can make mistakes and still have the possibility of repairing them. I can be okay even when no one is paying attention to me.

Today, I will be open to receiving the gift of humility.

Old man whose sperm swims in my veins,
come back in love, come back in pain.
— Toi Derricotte

A man who never knew his father said, "My father had no influence on me." Then, as he pondered that thought further, he realized his father had had a great influence on him by his absence. In fact, he had searched all his life to learn what his father was like and had often wondered if his father would be proud of him.

Many of us grew up feeling the absence of our fathers, either because they were physically gone or because they were emotionally disconnected from us. We patched together a youth in which we grew up and became adult men, but we continue to wonder about that man whose genes shape us. What was he like?

For some of us it is still possible, as grown men, to change our relationships with our fathers, to bring up personal topics with them, to ask about their lives. For many of us that isn't possible, but all of us can learn to live in better ways. We can now develop genuine personal relationships with other men who have real feelings. And we become happier, more courageous, and wholesome men by doing so.

Today, I will have a genuine personal
conversation with another man.

When I was small I was very naughty and my father chased me with his belt to give me a thrashing. Maybe that was how I got accustomed to running.
— Fermín Cacho, middle-distance runner

Not all bad things are all bad. All of us can look back at painful times and still say that we became better men for the experience. Men who have had cancer; men who spent years in prison, even unjustly accused; men who were abused—all have said that they used the experience to grow and improve. That is the sign of a good man.

Artists say that great design often occurs when they are forced to work within the limits of a situation. The outcome is not their original vision but an evolution into something surprising and wonderful. In this program, we hear the stories of many others who struggled with great challenges but used their struggles toward constructive results. A great runner doesn't become great because he was chased by his father with a belt, but because he used his experiences to make something positive out of it. Our recovery is an example of that very thing.

Today, I will seek ways to turn my challenges into creative responses.

Those who contemplate the beauty
of the earth find reserves of strength
that will endure as long as life lasts.
— *Rachel Carson*

Where do we turn for contemplation and contact with a spiritual source? Many men find it in nature. They look out the window at a handsome tree. They go for a walk outdoors, feed the birds, let themselves be awed by the sight of the moon on a dark night. The natural world offers our most direct, tangible contact with something eternal. We are part of something much larger than ourselves, something that endures for the ages.

The beauty of nature inspires awe, which is a form of reverence. We walk along a canyon rim and God is there. We walk through prairie grasses and wildflowers teeming with wildlife, the wind blows in our faces, and our spirits rise. These natural beauties endure forever.

Today, as I look at the natural world, I see God.

An error doesn't become a mistake
until you refuse to correct it.
—Orlando A. Battista

In our lives, we have always been drawn to extremes. If it isn't white, it must be black. If a little bit feels good, we take a lot. If we are going to do something, only perfection is good enough. So if we don't win, we lose, and if we can't do it perfectly, we feel like a failure.

In this program, we learn to seek progress, not perfection. And we can only make progress by trial and error. We learn nothing if we don't try new things and then learn from our errors. We don't jump into perfect sobriety the moment we decide to enter this program of recovery. When we surrender to our powerlessness over our addictions and codependency, we have to begin to learn how to live in a new way. It doesn't just happen all at once. So when we take our errors and our slips and agree to learn from them, we become stronger in our sobriety.

Today, I accept my imperfection as a
permanent condition, and I will keep
coming back to the program of recovery.

The first peace, which is the most important, is that which comes within the souls of people when they realize their relationship, their oneness, with the universe and all its powers, and when they realize that at the center of the universe dwells Wakan Tanka, and that this center is really everywhere, it is within each of us.

— *Black Elk*

When we understand power and powerlessness, we begin to find inner peace. We have often felt alone, isolated from others and from the world. Now we are learning about relationships and our connection to all things. Our biggest mistake was a childish notion that power and control are up to the individual. We didn't trust or even know about relationships and the forces of the universe.

We are actually part of an awesome universe, and we have a place in it. When we develop our relationships and understand our oneness with all others and the forces at work, we understand that we are never alone. We only participate in this big picture.

Today, I live as a relative to all people and the whole world.

The kid doesn't chew tobacco, smoke, drink,
curse, or chase broads. I don't see how he can
ever make it.

— *Richie Ashburn, former*
Major League Baseball player

We grew up with many misguided messages about what it takes to be a real man. These ideas were fun in some ways but led us down paths of self-defeating behavior. They gave us boyish ideas without pointing the way to genuinely strong and masculine lives. Now we know that a strong man has fun but still holds values such as honesty, kindness, and generosity.

Toughness is a virtue in many situations, but no one is more masculine than the guy with strength of character. A truly strong man lends a hand to others; he reflects daily on his own character and holds himself responsible. And he can be as sensual and playful as the best of them.

Today, I am grateful to be walking
on the path of a true masculine life.

Never let the fear of striking out get in your way.
— *Babe Ruth*

Fear is a normal emotion that many of us have to face. Some call it one of their character defects. We may have been more ruled by it than we admitted to ourselves. We allowed fear to be our guide when higher purposes told us we should make other choices. Because we honored our fears, we took refuge in controlling others, or in the fleeting ecstasies of our addictions. But that trap doesn't have to keep its grip on us. The best cure for fear is to confront it again and again. Fear of heights goes away when we repeatedly face high places.

Fear is just another emotion; it doesn't have to rule our choices. The best way to handle fear is to acknowledge the feeling and then put it in our back pocket while we move forward and do what we need to do. We also have the reassurance that we need not face anything alone. Our Higher Power is always with us. We focus on doing our best and turn the outcome over to the care of God *as we understand God*.

Today, I will acknowledge my fears,
pay attention to them, and then follow
the guidance of my higher purposes.

> *I have one request: may I never*
> *use my reason against truth.*
> — Elie Wiesel

Honesty with ourselves is a great asset in every situation we confront. The skill to look reality square in the face and call it what it is takes us a good distance toward coping with it. However, many of us also have the skill to spin or rationalize our actions so that we don't have to face something unpleasant. That skill provides us with excuses and evasions, but it is the greatest betrayal of our selves. When we use our brain to cleverly cover the truth of our actions, we often believe our own lies, and then they keep us stuck. Just as dishonesty builds and grows on itself, so does honesty. We cannot one day decide to be honest and change in a flash because we don't see all of our self-deceit yet. But we can make the decision to be as honest as we know how. Then we will soon be surprised by how much is revealed to us as the fog of our self-deceit lifts and our honesty builds on itself.

> *Today, I will strive to see reality as it is*
> *and not shape it to suit my ego's desires.*

JUNE

No matter what accomplishments you achieve,
somebody helps you.

— Althea Gibson

Some of us can get so full of ourselves when we win
a race or get a raise that we think we did it all by ourselves. But the question is, What is really so good about
the idea of doing it all by ourselves? Isn't it just as good
to achieve something great and give credit to all those
who helped us? We live in a community of friends and
neighbors; we are all part of a larger system that holds
us up. We have teachers and mentors who help us on
our way. We have doctors who help us keep our bodies
healthy. We have loved ones who support us and give
us more meaning in our lives.

During our active addiction, some of us were so
invested in the idea of fierce individualism that we deval-
ued anything that required help from others. That was a
limited and immature way of seeing things. The paradox
is that not until we could accept help could we gain the
strength required for a better life.

Today, I feel very proud of my accomplishments
and very grateful for all the help I had
in achieving them.

Always and never are two words you should
always remember never to use.
— *Wendell Johnson*

Words are powerful. We have a way of thinking in terms of all or nothing, black or white, and seldom in shades of gray. If we like something, we want more and more of it. If we take on a project, we throw ourselves into it with all we've got. But the truth is, life is mostly somewhere between extremes. If a little of something is good, more is not necessarily better. When we have a bad day, it doesn't mean that our whole life is a mess. If we say, "You always . . ." or "You never . . ." to a friend or loved one, the discussion is sure to intensify. If we use those words in conflict, the other person is sure to feel misunderstood. *Always* and *never* are extreme words that are rarely accurate. We are learning to live life in moderation and to think and see life more honestly.

Today, I will remember to see the shades of gray,
rather than the extremes of black and white.

Man's heart away from nature becomes hard.
— *Standing Bear*

The wisdom of Native American spirituality is deeply centered on the natural world. It teaches us to respect the earth and all natural things. It teaches us, as many world religions do, that we are made of earth and live by the gifts of nature. Remember, the word *humility* comes from the word *humus,* meaning "of the earth." When we become alienated or too far removed from nature, we become disconnected from ourselves. We lose our place and become willful.

Humility is not the same as shame. Humility is self-respecting, and it expresses that we have a place in the entire web of life. One aspect of a spiritual life is the feeling of awe. Where better to return to the feeling of awe than in sight of a mighty river, a powerful storm, or the intricate details of a flower or a stone.

Today, I will return to the natural world around me,
and with awe, I will give thanks.

*When it comes to staying young, a mind-lift
beats a face-lift any day.*

— Marty Bucella

We can choose to focus our attention on the image we
present to others, or to focus on who we are on the inside.
When we feel inadequate or empty, it may never occur to
us to do something about how we feel about ourselves.
Instead, we may have learned to try to control how others
see us—as if that were the path to self-esteem. In our
recovery, we learn that the basis of true self-esteem is to
have values and follow them. No matter how successful a man becomes economically, no matter how many
achievements he can point to in the world, it is never
enough until he feels right about himself as a person.

We can be grateful for a program that points the
way toward genuine success: true self-respect and self-
acceptance. That doesn't mean we never regret something we have done; it means we make distinctions
between who we are and what we have done. When we
have values and follow them, sometimes we fall short
of our own standards. Then we admit our shortcomings
and repair them. In so doing, our inner self-acceptance
is maintained and we once again affirm who we are.

*Today, I am more concerned about the man I am
than about the image I show to others.*

Wisdom doesn't necessarily come with age.
Sometimes age just shows up all by itself.
— Tom Wilson

If we live long enough, we will grow old. During that time, we will make plenty of mistakes and have plenty of opportunities to learn from them. However, sometimes we refuse to accept the lessons that are wrapped in our experience. We may be so determined to have what we want that we deny the truth of what we can actually have. We may be so prideful or so stubborn or so insecure that we defy the lessons we are being taught and refuse to open ourselves to a new idea. We grow older, but not smarter.

Some men become very grown-up and very strong in wisdom at a young age. They are blessed with an open, engaging attitude and a willingness to surrender to truth when it faces them. We should cultivate an attitude of learning, of openness to new lessons, and of willingness to learn the lessons taught by our mistakes.

Today, I will learn from my experience
and become a little stronger and a little wiser.

*Defeat may serve as well as victory to shake
the soul and let the glory out.*
— *Edwin Markham*

No one goes in search of a defeat so that he can have a
stirring spiritual experience. The real defeats are the ones
that we would never choose. They shake our foundations
and give us a changed life to deal with. They force us to
see things from an angle we never saw before. We start
from the empty feeling and the question: "Now what?"
Defeat is inevitable in life. We aren't really adults until we
have confronted situations that we desperately wanted
to conquer but could not. It is in learning to accept the
reality of powerlessness that we have the first opportunity to become full adults. When a man stops at defeat
and feels only defeated, without finding the wisdom to
grow beyond it, he stays stuck in that spot. In recovery
and healing, we are learning that the renewed life that
comes after we accept our powerlessness is full of possibilities—and a serenity we didn't know before.

*Today, I am grateful for the adult perspective
I gained from acknowledging a reality
that I could not control.*

Not all who wander are lost.
— *J. R. R. Tolkien*

We are wandering on a path. We are able to look back and see how far we have come, and perhaps we can see some distance ahead. But we are exploring what a recovered life means. We cannot predict what will happen in the future, and we cannot see what is around the next bend. Some people respond to the unknown with fear. On the spiritual path we are following, we put fear in our back pocket. We continue to wander while practicing the principle of turning our lives and our will over to the care of God. There is no need to fear. We know that we will face challenges and that we will not be alone.

Since we cannot foresee what will happen in the future, we can only know that we will meet whatever happens with our best self. Life is an adventure. The difference between fear and excitement is the knowledge that our Higher Power will be with us. We have our friends; we have our honesty and our self-respect. Even though we don't know what is around the next turn, we are not lost.

Today, I am grateful to be in the
care of my Higher Power.

We do not err because truth is difficult
to see. It is visible at a glance. We err
because this is more comfortable.
—Aleksandr Solzhenitsyn

When we are directed to make a "searching and fearless moral inventory of ourselves," it is because in our old ways we looked for the more comfortable answers. Honesty with ourselves can be uncomfortable when we first let ourselves in on the secrets we kept away from our consciousness. We see things we do not want to look at. We may have long-held patterns of shaping and softening the facts so we could continue our harmful and self-abusive ways. And as we lied to and betrayed ourselves, we made ourselves weaker and less able to deal with our situation.

Now we value honesty with ourselves. Honesty may be uncomfortable, but it will not hurt us. Once we have the courage to be honest with ourselves, we don't have to decide immediately what we will do with what we see. We can take it in steps. First, we admit what we know to be true—and then we can live with what we know for a while. Slowly wisdom will grow within us, and we will more clearly see a path for how to proceed.

Today, I will not shy away from
honesty with myself.

The fastest way to freedom
is to feel your feelings.
— Gita Bellin

Many of us were taught in boyhood that feelings should
be avoided. Some men think that any kind of vulnerability should be hidden, and most feelings can make us feel
vulnerable. For some of us, the only acceptable feeling
is the one that makes us feel stronger: anger. Many men
don't even know what their feelings are; many others
recognize their feelings but have never learned how to
express them to others. When we found our addictions
and codependencies, they quickly became handy ways to
hide from feelings. But that only served our false sense
of masculinity.

As we seek a life free from compulsions and addictions, moving from the foolish ways to the wise ways
of true manhood, we honestly admit our feelings. We
are strong enough to stop hiding. We honestly feel our
feelings because they allow us to live more fully.

Today, I will be conscious of my feelings
and give them a place in my life.

I felt angry toward my friend.
I told my wrath. My wrath did end.
I felt angry toward my foe.
I told him not. My wrath did grow.
— William Blake

A basic fact of our human nature is that expressing our feelings helps resolve them. When we push them down or keep them hidden, we preserve them and save them up, and sometimes the pressure only makes them grow. Many of us are afraid that expressing our feelings will make things worse. We have learned that we are capable of suppressing our feelings to smooth situations over. However, those feelings come out later, either through uncontrolled outrage or as problems with our health.

A good relationship only grows deeper and more trusting when we express our feelings to each other. It may feel awkward or risky to tell a loved one that we feel hurt, but when we say it respectfully, we can expect a respectful reply. When we have good methods of communication, our relationships grow stronger and deeper with each passing year.

When I feel anger, I will express it respectfully.

In everyone's heart stirs a great homesickness.
— Rabbi Seymour Siegel

We ask ourselves what drove us to do some of the things we did. We went to extremes when we knew our actions were not rational. Even today, we are drawn to extremes. At times, we still long for things that we know will hurt us. Are we puzzled by these desires?

Wise men and prophets have searched their own deep truths to understand their desires and longings. Many say that our desires and hungers are, at the base of our being, a search for a spiritual home, a place where we know we are welcome, safe, and loved. Perhaps we are all born longing for that home. Maybe we first taste it when we first experience the warmth of loving and caring parents, even when it was only a taste, and only partially satisfied. Then we spend the rest of our lives in pursuit of that good feeling again. The wisdom of the Twelve Steps points us toward that spiritual home. A lifetime of growth and development follows in which we feel the spirit in our fellowship with other men and women, and we learn from others how they have found their way home.

Today, the stirring in my heart will be
a sign of my spiritual longing.

*When the truth is told lovingly, with insight
and compassion, you can say anything.*
— *Shawnee Undell*

There are times when we know something, or we have a difficult thing to say to someone, and we can't see how we could possibly speak it. Perhaps today our spouse or dear friend has done something we feel upset about, or perhaps someone at work is doing something that we need to discuss with him or her.

When we have a hard message to deliver, we don't have to speak it harshly. We can say almost anything to someone if we can put our arm around that person, figuratively speaking. Naturally, we can't always expect to be received with open arms when our message is hard to hear. A sensitive or painful truth sometimes is the valuable gift that only we as friends can deliver. We don't even have to be right; what is required is that we are sincere.

*Today, I will look for loving and
compassionate ways to say my truth.*

To the rationally minded, the mental processes
of the intuitive appear to work backward. His
conclusions are reached before his premises.
— Frances G. Wickes

Intuition is a valuable form of wisdom that often seems mystical. We lose our keys and can't find them in any of the usual places, and then an idea pops into our mind about where to find them. When we look there, we find them. Only after the fact can we explain—maybe—why that spot came to mind. That's intuition. Or, on a higher plane, we have a feeling that a certain choice in our life would be a big mistake, or one day, for no clear reason, we expect our partner to tell us something important.

The wisdom of our intuition deserves our great respect. It is a valuable guide. Even though it is not 100 percent accurate, and we cannot expect it to be, we should not violate ourselves by contradicting it. Instead, we grow by developing our intuition, listening to what we imagine and what we feel, and following our instincts. Intuition is another form of spiritual strength.

Today, I will listen to my inner feelings
about things, even when I don't immediately
understand them rationally.

Life is what happens to you when
you're busy making other plans.
— *John Lennon*

We have plans and dreams about our future. We hope to accomplish certain goals in our lives. Maybe we want to buy a house or get a promotion. We have a future with our life partner, or we are looking for a life partner. But life is never so cut-and-dried that we should expect everything to go according to our plans. We live better and healthier if we hold loosely to our anticipations; the path we walk in reality is never the exact path we envisioned. Life is an adventure in which sometimes things turn out even better than we hoped, and sometimes we have to cope with great disappointments.

Surprisingly, after we deal with the unexpected, we are often grateful for what it brought or what we learned. How often have we heard someone say he is grateful for the way an illness changed his life, or the way a great loss taught him to be a better person? Perhaps today we have to face a difficult challenge or manage a problem that we would never have chosen. The difficulty that we face is part of our unique life journey, and if we allow it to, it will guide us toward becoming a better man.

Today, I will make my plans and still be
willing to deal with whatever happens.

When a man's willing and eager, the gods join in.
— *Aeschylus*

We can learn a lot about our present state of mind by asking ourselves what we are willing and eager for. Just now, are we willing to know ourselves better? Do we seek to become better human beings? Are we willing to move beyond self-destructive desires and leave them behind? Or are we more willing and eager for someone else to make things easy for us? Are we still holding on to our desires for control? Do we still hold on to hope for another ecstatic high?

After we face ourselves with the truth of what we really want, the truth can change us. First, we are honest with ourselves, and that boosts our ability to actively choose what we really want. When we become willing, we are ready for the work of our Higher Power to help us go where we want to go.

Today, I will keep in mind what I really want
and not become distracted by temptations
that lead off the path.

Loss *is another word for* change.
— *M. Tating*

We don't always realize how loss and grief are natural parts of life. Every change contains a loss within it. If we get a job promotion, we lose some elements of our work that are familiar and maybe enjoyable. If we get married, we lose the independence of the single life. If we choose recovery, we lose the friends we had in our addiction and codependency. And, of course, when we lose a loved one, the changes that follow are never chosen, but they may actually lead us toward new possibilities.

Surprisingly, every loss, every grief, has embedded within it the gift of a new beginning. In the midst of our losses, we can seldom see the gift. We don't want to lose what we love. And grief is a necessary part of letting go. Grief is the wail of pain that comes when we know we must let go. And then life goes on. There is life after loss! It is a changed life. Perhaps nothing will ever be the same as it was. But it can become a new stage of our life, deeper and richer, even though we never could have imagined it.

Today, I embrace change,
even knowing it means some loss.

A word from the heart goes straight to the heart.
— Henri Huvelin

When we have something important to tell someone, we may feel afraid of how it will be received. Or when a friend experiences a tragedy, we may wonder what to say: this kind of situation can throw us into retreat mode and leave us silent. Or maybe we carry secrets we wish we could share, but we don't dare to speak. It's reassuring to recall the times when people have said important things to us. Their sincerity always meant more than any particular words they used.

Our message always contains more than just words. The very fact that we let someone into our confidence is a compliment. The fact that we care enough to show our feelings is a message of trust. When we give that kind of compliment to someone, we have a right to expect it to be treated gently, as a gift.

Today, in my personal relationships,
I will speak from my heart.

Life is a great big canvas, and you should throw all the paint on it you can.
— Danny Kaye

Our recovery started because of unmanageability and loss of control. That was a very frightening state of life. However, if simply abstaining was our entire goal, we would become very suppressed and limited beings. Our need for caution and control would become pervasive in our lives. That is where a dry drunk is stuck. A successful and happy recovery brings freedom, peace of mind, and self-esteem. We learn how to relax and enjoy life to its fullest because we no longer have to be so concerned with control. We can release our deeper selves to engage freely in the wholesome and healthy pleasure of friendships, love and sex, family connections, good food, sports and recreation, and fulfilling work.

We don't have to hold back our enthusiasm for life any longer. We are free to release our playfulness and take risks because we have a safe base in our Higher Power and our program. We can imagine trips we want to take, we can let our intuition speak to us, and we can dream of things we want to do and make plans to fulfill them.

Today, I will paint freely on the canvas before me.

To have more, desire less.
—*Anonymous*

So many of us are caught up in such a busy pace of life that we feel we don't have time for the basic things like dinner with our family, time to talk to our intimate partner, or quiet time to unwind and reflect. What is the problem? Often the problem is that we are caught in a never-ending search for more material things than our income can comfortably afford. In modern life, we are daily subjected to well-crafted advertising that tells us we would be happy if we bought another alluring item. Turning aside from those seductions, deciding we can live more comfortably if we seek happiness elsewhere, frees us from that demanding cycle.

If we examine our desires, we will quickly recognize that we already have enough material goods. Happiness, gratitude, and peace of mind will come from the abundance of our relationships and the knowledge that we are the kind of men we hope to be. We can limit our desires for more goods and free ourselves from the feeling that we don't have enough.

Today, I will remind myself that I have enough.
I am grateful for the abundance in my life.

> *A great teacher never strives to explain
> his vision—he simply invites you to stand
> beside him and see for yourself.*
> — *Reverend R. Inman*

In the spirit of our recovering fellowship, we are very
cautious about advising anyone. Advice is only given
when requested and even then with great care. Words
of advice are so easily spoken but so often off target. We
all find it easy to see what someone else should do, but
the much harder task is to find insight into our own
actions. So we focus on the harder and more helpful
part, striving to live our lives as well as possible. We
can grow by standing beside other successful recovering
people and learning how they do it, and we can allow
others to stand beside us to learn what they can. A good
example is always the best teacher. The wisest men are
not sure their advice is useful to anyone. They just live
their lives in ways that suit them, and others can take
from it whatever is useful and leave the rest.

*Today, I will work on the harder task of deepening
my insight into my own thoughts and actions.*

Do not let a little dispute
injure a great friendship.
— H. Jackson Brown Jr.

There are many kinds of friends. Some are work friends; we enjoy knowing each other and doing our jobs but don't ever get very personal. We have recreational friends with whom we enjoy doing the same activities. Some friends are like soul mates; we feel we were cut from the same cloth, and we understand each other at a deep level. With our soul mates we can talk about almost anything—and sometimes we don't have to talk about it. And some friends are lifelong buddies who knew us way back when; we know each other in ways that new friends never can.

Our egos can get in the way and spoil the development of good friendships. For instance, we may take things too personally and feel offended over small things. Or sometimes our ego may be so determined to be right that we sacrifice the friendship in order to stand up for our position. A good friendship requires that our ego step back a bit, making room for others to have dignity and be imperfect too.

Today, I am grateful for all the different
kinds of friends in my life.

*A man of faith does not bargain
or stipulate with God.*
— Mahatma Gandhi

When we finally admitted that we were powerless over the substance or behavior of our addiction or codependency, we had already covered a lot of ground. Most of us had suffered great personal despair, defeat, and self-hate before we could see our problem for what it was. As the Big Book of Alcoholics Anonymous says, we, too, had tried to "find an easier, softer way. But we could not." We bargained with ourselves and with nature, saying we would cut back or we would abstain for a period of time. Nothing short of total, unconditional acceptance of our powerlessness could release us from the grips of our problem.

The paradox of this surrender to reality didn't strike us until later. Surrender to the truth is liberating. As long as we admit our powerlessness daily and never again try to bargain ourselves into a position of control, we are free to become the kind of men we respect and to have the respect of those we love.

*Today, once again, as if for the first time, I admit
my powerlessness and throw myself on the grace
of my Higher Power to restore my spirit.*

I'm as pure as the driven slush.
— *Tallulah Bankhead*

There is something to be said for claiming our imperfection and wearing it proudly. There is so much more
freedom and health in imperfection than in the stifling
and unreal drive to be perfect. When we decide to put
the shame and dishonor of our misbehaviors behind us,
we are tempted to think that the opposite extreme would
be better, but it is not. Instead of striving to be perfect, let
us accept our imperfection. Instead of trying to climb to
the top of the ladder of perfect actions, let us accept that
we will make mistakes and that no honest man will ever
reach that point. Let us strive instead to keep returning
to our standards.

Many of us have said that living one day at a time is too
much for us. We tell ourselves that we are just going to
live this day, but a half hour later we are worrying again
about the future. We have to keep reminding ourselves to
live one minute or one hour at a time. That is the attitude
we adopt when we accept our imperfection. Instead of
expecting to hold to our standards perfectly, we simply
keep returning to them.

*Today, I embrace my imperfection, and when
I veer off course, I will keep returning to my path.*

It is well to remind ourselves that anxiety signi-
fies a conflict, and so long as a conflict is going
on, a constructive solution is possible.
— *Rollo May*

Anxiety is a sign of life. All living things experience it;
it is nothing to be feared. In fact, we double our anxiety
if we are afraid of our feelings of fear. Anxious feelings
may be a guide, an intuition pointing us in a direction
we need to follow. They can direct us away from some
situations and toward others. They may be a sign that we
have neglected something or that an important matter
remains unfinished.

When we become familiar with our feelings, we also
become more comfortable with them. We welcome them
like friends who tell us what we need to pay attention
to. One way to become more aware of our feelings is to
just pause and quietly breathe with slow, deep breaths.
In that simple physical act, our bodies quiet down, and
we can think more clearly.

Today, I will give my anxiety its rightful place
rather than fighting it, and I will pay attention
to its message.

*Baseball teaches us, or has taught most of us,
how to deal with failure. We learn at a very
young age that failure is the norm in baseball
and . . . errors [are] part of the game, part of
its rigorous truth.*

— *Francis T. Vincent Jr.*

Of course, we will make mistakes. We are born with the
right to make mistakes. There is no shame in that. Perfection is a false ideal for a real human being. We learn by
trial and error. If we try to be perfect, we will meet dead
ends and roadblocks because we will inevitably fall short.

Instead, there is wisdom in the motto "Keep coming
back." In this instance, the motto refers to returning to
our standards. Rather than to strive constantly for higher
and higher perfection, our goal is to always return to
the rules we live by. Of course, we will veer off the path.
When we do, we make repairs, pay our dues, and hold
our place as full-fledged members of the human race.

*Today, my goal is to keep returning
to my ethics for a good life.*

I've had a wonderful time but this wasn't it.
— *Groucho Marx*

How often we went out in search of pleasure to escape our problems, and our desires only led us into much bigger problems. Alcohol, gambling, sex, food, and even taking care of others are all pleasures. They have been part of good times in many people's lives. But we know that pursuit of these pleasures can be abused and create only heartache and sickness.

In this program, we are dealing with the age-old problem of how to manage our desires. This is a spiritual problem. We are born with desires. Our development into strong manhood is partly a growth in our ability to learn from experience and choose how and when to satisfy these desires—and which ones are best left unsatisfied. We are learning that a hearty, healthy man can live very well with some desires unfulfilled.

Today, I will have a wonderful time,
in part, because I choose to leave some
desires and impulses unsatisfied.

*But they that wait upon the Lord shall renew
their strength; they shall mount up with wings
as eagles; they shall run, and not be weary; and
they shall walk, and not faint.*

— Isaiah 40:31

The Third Step tells us that the path of recovery includes
a "decision to turn our will and our lives over to the care
of God *as we understood Him.*" This step presents a paradox: turning our lives and will over to the care of our
Higher Power in fact inspires us with greater strength.

Our own life stories, and the stories of healing and
recovery that we hear from our friends and our mentors,
illustrate this biblical wisdom. Our lives were a mess. We
tried to control more than a man can control, and we
ended up out of control. The losses we paid were painful
and heartbreaking. But when we chose to enter into a
spiritual recovery, we felt we had rejoined the human
family. We were inspired with a new sense of hope and
energy and possibilities for our lives.

*Today, again, I turn to my Higher Power
for the care of my life and my will.*

It is perfectly true, as philosophers say,
that life must be understood backwards.
But they forget the other proposition,
that it must be lived forwards.
— *Søren Kierkegaard*

Real life presents us with unexpected puzzles and challenges. Like going on a trip, part of the reason for going is to experience the unexpected. Looking forward on our path, we see bends and turns ahead, and we don't know what's around them. So we look forward to them with a mixture of anticipation and concern.

This adventure of life deepens with the understanding we get from our past experiences. What we have already learned sharpens our skills for dealing with today, and still we will meet new surprises, and we will continue to learn. Even though we have no control over what appears on our path, there is no need for fear or panic because we have turned our lives over to the care of our Higher Power. We will learn how to deal with it.

Today, I rely on what I have learned about life,
and I trust in God to support me.

We only have one person to blame,
and that's each other.
— *Barry Beck, NHL player*

Blame is not a word that works well for us. It is an attack word, a negative assault that fails to point toward anything better. Much better is the word *responsible*. When a man opens a door and accidentally knocks down a child on the other side, he is responsible for his action, and he reaches down to help the child up again. It is nothing to be ashamed of or blamed for. He isn't a bad person for doing that. But he takes responsibility.

Blame and responsibility are difficult matters for us to separate. Many of us have felt blamed and shamed from our earliest memories. As a result, when we are responsible, we have a knee-jerk impulse to feel ashamed. But taking responsibility without shame is what a strong man does. We can learn to separate them, and as we do, our self-esteem rises.

Today, I will take responsibility for my actions
and respect myself for doing so.

The man who has no imagination has no wings.
— *Muhammad Ali*

The most important creative project we have is our own lives, and imagination is a rich inner resource to guide us. We can develop our imagination if we give ourselves permission to dream and to let go of the bonds of reality and our immediate situation.

If I could be anywhere in the world right now, where would I want to be? What would I be doing? Who would be there with me? If I took a break from all my responsibilities for a day, what would I do with the day? What is it like to be another person, such as my best friend, my boss, my child? How would I most like to celebrate my next birthday? If today were the last day of my life, how would I want to live this day? If I could accomplish only one more thing in my life, what would I choose?

Today, I will let my thoughts take wing and fly into the creative world of imagination.

JULY

The past has flown away. The coming
month and year do not exist; ours only
is the present's tiny point.
— *Mahmud Shabestari*

We are tempted to look back and to look ahead. But what we most need to do is be present in this moment, with ourselves, with our loved ones and friends, and with our experience right here and right now. When we were lost and asleep in our using days and codependency, we could not be emotionally present. Our thoughts were taken up with how we would get our next drink, our next big gambling win, or our next sexual exploit—or with how to handle the latest crisis. To be emotionally present and live in the moment takes time, and it's a frame of mind that develops as we grow in recovery.

One way we become more present in the moment is to practice gratitude. We can always name a few things we feel grateful for: small and big things, funny and serious things. Looking through the lens of gratitude brings us into the immediate moment.

Today, I will look at my day
through the lens of gratitude.

My life is in the hands of any fool
who makes me lose my temper.
— Joseph Hunter

Many of us have learned that we can get a real buzz from anger. It seems to give us direct access to our egos, where we feel an inflated sense of power and entitlement. We no longer feel vulnerable; we see things in black-and-white terms. We believe we are right. But in this primitive state of excitement, we are reacting from the animal level, and our grown-up brain has been bypassed. This kind of habitual reaction can leave a lot of damage in its aftermath. It undermines our dearest relationships and our own self-respect.

We need to examine our patterns with anger. We don't seek to be rid of it but to manage it as grown men. Do we take responsibility for staying honest in the midst of anger? Can we hold on to our humility while being angry? When we express angry feelings, do we avoid abusive words and intimidating actions? We can feel our anger and express it without reverting to our primitive brain.

Today, I will be aware of angry feelings
and express them with a clear sense
of my grown-up masculinity.

To err is human; to blame it on the
other guy is even more human.
— *Bob Goddard*

We are on a path that leads us to become better men. A central theme on this path is learning to take responsibility for ourselves, our mistakes, and our choices as we deal with our situation. We can make progress on this path by noticing our defensive reactions when we make a mistake or when someone criticizes us. Our old ways were aimed at shifting the blame or counterattacking. Now we are learning how to take on the blame when it honestly belongs to us.

One of the first things we need to learn in taking responsibility is that there is no shame in making a mistake. Everyone makes mistakes. But some people don't accept responsibility for them, and others do. We have much greater respect for someone who does. Admitting when we were wrong doesn't mean speaking in vague generalities, saying that "mistakes were made." It doesn't mean saying, "Yes, I did this, but only because you did that." It means saying what we did or didn't do and laying the facts out there for us and others to deal with. When we can do that, forgiveness almost always follows shortly.

Today, I will hold back my defensiveness
and admit the facts as they are.

A community is like a ship; everyone
ought to be prepared to take the helm.
— Henrik Ibsen

A good life is blessed with many communities. There are neighborhoods, schools, synagogues, churches, mosques, groups of friends, workplaces, and Twelve Step recovery groups. We became alienated from our communities when we were attached to our addictions and codependency. The all-consuming demands of our misguided lives left little room for genuine participation in the human network.

On our path, we now treasure these connections. We are participants in the bonds of warmth and the many good relationships that surround us. We don't have to be the center of attention or the main focus in order to feel included. We contribute to the networks that we are part of by simply being good men, and by taking our share of the duties that make a better community for us all.

Today, I will seek to make a positive contribution
to the communities in my life.

Some people are so afraid to die
that they never begin to live.
— *Henry Van Dyke*

Fear is a dirty word for most guys. We find it hard to admit the truth. But the truth is, in our denial of fear we have often been ruled by it. We certainly know the fear of going without the comfort we had in our addictive and codependent ways. Our anxiety was hidden under our controlling behaviors when we said, "I'm only doing it because I love you," or "I'm only going to take a little hit." Many of us have felt so alone and grew up in such a stressful world that we learned to be constantly on guard against danger, even as we denied our fears.

Life inherently involves risk. There is such a thing as too much control. In its ultimate form, control is static and dead. That is why spiritual awakening is so central to our healing and recovery. We can stay spiritually alive, aware of life's risks but remaining calm. When we fear what this day will bring, or what the future holds, we place our fears in the hands of God as we understand God. What happens next is beyond rational explanation, but it lets us go forward without grasping for our old self-destructive comforts.

Today, I will admit that I feel fear as any man does,
and I stay calm in the care of God.

You're never too old to grow up.
— *Shirley Conran*

A child's view of adults is that they have arrived at some fixed point where they are emancipated and have all the tools necessary for life. An adult knows that we never stop growing. Many of us have been stuck in an immature level of development. Our life stresses and our addictions took us off the track of emotional growth. We found substitutes and evasions for truly dealing with the normal life problems. Now we are back on the much more rewarding path of truly living and growing.

We accept the adult wisdom that we all need help and we all continue to learn and grow throughout our life span. We finally feel like adults because we take responsibility for our actions. We don't blame others for our problems, and when our days feel challenging, we can ask for help. Back on our path, we are never alone.

*Today, I am grateful to be on the path
of dealing with my life and continuing
to grow truly stronger.*

· JULY 7 ·

It is the wounded oyster that
mends its shell with pearl.
— *Ralph Waldo Emerson*

Many of us felt like outsiders in the past. As children, we
weren't in the most popular group, or we were picked
last when teams were chosen. And almost everyone has
been picked on sometimes. As adults, our wounds may
have been self-inflicted, but no less painful for that. The
key question today is, Are we still on a track that creates
more wounds, or are we on the mend?

There is great spiritual benefit to knowing what it feels
like to be a wounded person. It provides the resource that
many great men have built their wisdom and perspective
on. We all know men we admire deeply who have come
through hard and painful times, not knowing how it
would all turn out. They followed this path of healing
and spiritual growth and, because of their healing, have
become men of the highest quality.

Today, I can see my past wounds as a source
for spiritual and emotional strength.

Victory is in the quality of competition,
not the final score.
                                    — *Mike Marshall*

Competition is neither good nor bad. It is like any other force that can be used in good ways or bad. For us, winning means being the kind of man we most admire. When we are in a competitive game, whether it is in athletics, business, or a friendly discussion, we strive first to compete in ways that we respect. We don't give up our moral or human values in order to come out with the top score at the end. We don't indulge in hate or anger at the other guy simply because he is our competition at the moment. We play fair, we respect others, and we enjoy a good and worthy competitor.

Keeping our eye on the ball means we stay focused on what we are truly trying to win. That is a kind of wisdom that we weren't born with; we develop it through conscious effort and attention. Today, we certainly face some competitive situations, whether it is engaging with a particular co-worker or someone with an opposing viewpoint in a group we are part of. At the end of the day, if we have our values intact, we will have won our best prize.

Today, I will be a strong and
honorable competitor.

Don't go around saying the world owes you a living. The world owes you nothing. It was here first.
— Mark Twain

Some men have a very passive attitude about their life. While they may seem to have a lot of bravado, they feel dependent on the inside and look to others to supply what they need. When it doesn't come, they feel hurt, neglected, and angry. Others see their life as a gift from the beginning. Opportunities may be more or less available, but they use what they have to create a life that has meaning. They don't settle for negative thinking, and they develop a rewarding inner world.

We can change our attitude toward our lives. All of us have some unproductive, negative thoughts that only keep us stuck. Perhaps we have old resentments that burden our days, or we hold on to old debts that could never be repaid. To free ourselves to live fully, we can consciously and deliberately reshape these thoughts. We can shift our attention from what we don't have to what is possible now.

Today, I am grateful for the gift of life, and I will take my life and grow from here.

The significant problems we face cannot
be solved at the same level of thinking we
were at when we created them.
— *Albert Einstein*

Many of us stubbornly hold on to our long-established, preferred ways of looking at things. We don't think we are stubborn, only that we rely on what worked for us in the past. Perhaps as young guys, we coped with stress by keeping our thoughts to ourselves, or we figured out that we wouldn't get hurt if we didn't trust anyone. All the patterns that we developed as youngsters were our best attempts at the time to deal with our lives. The greater the stress we felt, the harder won were our coping responses, and the stronger our attachment to them.

Our best answers from boyhood may not fit our lifetimes as men. Holding too dearly to childhood solutions freezes us in immature and weaker levels of growth. What was charming and harmless behavior in a child can be manipulating and dishonest in a man. Thus, we create new problems. We need to let ourselves become more vulnerable—to give up the security of our old ways and open ourselves to the messages coming from our friends, our program, and our experiences.

Today, I will be open to insecurity and create
the possibility of growing stronger.

We couldn't conceive of a miracle
if none had ever happened.
— *Libbie Fudim*

We are very familiar with miracles. We see the change
that has happened in our own lives and in the lives of
others on this journey with us. Something deep within
us changed when we first decided we could accept the
truth of our powerlessness and the help of a Higher
Power. When a man's personality changes profoundly,
that is a miracle.

These transformations go beyond what anyone might
rationally expect. Some of us had given up and were
without hope. Others had given up on us too. We thought
our lives could never be different after we lived so long in
the grips of codependency and addiction, after we tried
in so many ways to manage and control our actions and
repeatedly failed. But this program provided an awakening, as if from a deep sleep or perhaps a nightmare. Now
we have found a path that produces genuine miracles. We
cannot easily explain it, but our compulsions are lifted.

Today, I am grateful for the miracle in my
own life and the lives of my friends.

Before talking of holy things, we prepare our-
selves by offering. . . . One will fill his pipe and
hand it to the other who will light it and offer it
to the sky and the earth. . . . They will smoke
together. . . . Then we will be ready to talk.
— Mato-Kuwapi, Santee Yankton Sioux

Rituals prepare us for moments of spiritual experience.
They bring people together; they mark occasions; they
give us metaphors through our senses that expose us to
mystery, awe, peace, and wisdom. Traditional spiritual
practices all use ritual to reach toward God. In our meetings, we also have rituals that accomplish these things.

We may have dismissed ritual in our cynical minds,
thinking of it as irrelevant hocus-pocus. But when we
seek connection with other people, or with God, we learn
that ritual is a way to set our cynical minds aside and
open ourselves to the presence. Even in our private time
of prayer and meditation, we may light a candle as a sign
of our spiritual search.

Today, I will honor the rituals
that create conscious contact.

*I don't ask for the meaning of the song of a bird
or the rising of the sun on a misty morning. There
they are, and they are beautiful.*

— Pete Hamill

Nature is the mystical, spiritual miracle present all around us every day. A walk in the woods or a hike in a park provides us with abundant evidence that we are part of something much bigger than ourselves. No one sent the bird to sing its song; no person designed a tree and planned its leaves to come forth. They are just doing their own thing. Our whole world is generously decorated by spontaneous beauty, and our senses take them in at no cost.

When we feel burdened by our problems and when we are too focused on ourselves, a walk outdoors will surely lighten the load. We can feel the wind in our face, look up at the sky and see the big and ever-changing heavens, or lie on the ground and feel the support of the earth. It is always a good practice to turn to the natural world when we feel the need for spiritual refreshment.

*Today, I will get outside myself by
noticing the eternal world of nature.*

*How much more grievous are the consequences
of anger than the causes of it.*
— Marcus Aurelius

Anger shatters our calm. Some of us show it in loud
bursts; others just quietly stew. Sometimes we feel angry
inside but we still want to look kind and unperturbed,
so our anger comes out sideways, hurting someone
indirectly or in sneaky ways. We all have felt the pangs
of regret after we said or did something in anger. We
wish we could magically turn back the clock and undo
the moment, gather up the pieces, and put them back
together again.

No one can simply banish the basic human emotion
of anger from his life. To be responsible, we must accept
our anger. It arises from within us, and handling it is our
own responsibility, even when we are perfectly justified
in feeling angry. We choose our way to express it. It is
never responsible to say, "You made me angry, so it's your
fault that I blew up."

After accepting our anger, we strive to develop a space
between the feeling and our actions. We learn to notice
our feelings before they reach the explosion point. In that
mental space, we choose how to express them.

*Today, I will notice and accept my anger,
then choose respectful ways to express it.*

We haven't needed to direct our minds consciously all that much until now, and we haven't really understood the delicacy and absolute necessity of doing so—until now.
— Robert Ornstein

When we are highly alert to this very moment and we feel the importance of focusing our conscious minds, we are in a spiritual space. Our spiritual development grows along these lines—we become more and more skilled at centering our senses and our consciousness in this moment. This is how our calmness and serenity grow.

We know that our health and survival depend on our spiritual growth. It is urgent for us, and for those we love, that we become better, more serene men. We can practice this by always being mindful of the concrete truths around us, and by doing just one thing at a time. When we eat, we are aware of the flavors and textures of our food. When we wash the dishes, we focus our mind on just washing the dishes. Multi-tasking does not advance our spiritual growth or serenity. Calmness comes when we focus our minds and allow all distractions to fall away.

Today is the day I am alive, and in this day I will practice focusing my consciousness.

Man is harder than iron, stronger than
stone and more fragile than a rose.
— *Turkish saying*

It is a boy's idea of a real man that leaves no room for softness or weakness. In his view, a real man is either strong or weak, either tough or soft. But a boy is not yet a man, and he can only imitate grown men. As we develop into adults with real life experience, and as we get to know ourselves with honesty, we no longer have to view our masculinity as a caricature. We know that our true nature contains both toughness and gentleness. When we are at peace with ourselves, we don't have to hide our gentleness to prove that we are strong.

We no longer have to prove anything. We have self-acceptance, including the whole complex mixture of elements that make up our character. And with self-acceptance, we don't need to focus on the image we portray to others. We just let ourselves be and express the truth of how we feel and who we are. That is the sign of a real man who has grown up.

Today, I am growing in self-knowledge,
and I accept myself as a complex mixture.

Courage is the price that life
exacts for granting peace.
— *Amelia Earhart*

We admire a man who bravely faces danger and does battle for a worthy cause. When courage fails a man, when he steps aside from the battle that needs to be fought, we feel that he missed his calling.

Recovery requires this kind of courage. In fact, the struggles with ourselves and with our inner demons are far more frightening than duking it out with a real live foe. We might get a thrill from the danger of driving fast, or climbing a rock wall, or skiing a challenging slope, yet we freeze when we try to talk about our feelings or make amends for a bad mistake.

The very act of beginning our recovery took courage. We put it off as long as we could. The battle seemed so frightening. When we could see no other escape, we raised the courage to go forward toward a worthwhile goal. And the peace that we have now is the reward for our courage.

Today, I pray for the courage to do
what I am called to do.

The mind creates the abyss
and the heart crosses it.
— Nisargadatta Maharaj

Sometimes we are filled with fear. The challenges facing us seem so large, and we feel so confused or so stymied. We wake in the middle of the night, and the worst images rise up in our thoughts. Our problems, real or imagined, can overwhelm us. We feel bereft and alone.

Yet, honestly, we don't have to live the whole future in one day, and we don't have to deal with everything alone. When running a long distance, we may feel tired and can't imagine continuing to the end. Yet we know we can keep running now, and we can keep taking step after step. We don't have to expend all of our energy in one burst. Our energy rebuilds along the path, even as we expend it. So it is with meeting the challenges of our lives. We take heart in knowing that we only have to deal with today. We are never alone because our creator is always with us.

Today, I will cross over any
difficulty I must face.

Eternity is a terrible thought. I mean,
where's it going to end?
                                        — *Tom Stoppard*

Looking at the stars on a clear night or the vastness of
the open sea gives us a sense of how small we are. It
may feel frightening to contemplate—and at the same
time comforting. What are we but a bit of earth sparked
to life by a force we didn't initiate? This rich mixture of
fear, comfort, and awe is what we can call spirituality.

In our program of recovery, we are guided to a spiritual path. The very search for a sense of meaning is a
spiritual quest. We are told to have faith in the God of
our understanding, and the paradox is that God is beyond
our understanding. God exceeds the confines of a human
definition. When we can relax into that realization, we
find comfort in the vastness, and we focus on being the
best kind of man we know how to be.

I can be at peace, knowing that what is
eternal exceeds my understanding.

*The trouble with not having a goal is that
you can spend your life running up and
down the field and never scoring.*
— Bill Copeland

We all have goals. Some of them are implicit or even
beneath our conscious awareness. Some of us have very
clear goals that we have spelled out for ourselves. Perhaps we are seeking to hold a certain job someday. Maybe
we have the goal of saving money for our children's col-
lege fund. Another goal might be to complete a particular
next Step in our recovery program.

It helps to spell out a few goals that we truly want to
accomplish. Sitting down and writing just a few goals
helps us find direction. That kind of list is best when it
is kept short, limited to a few things we sincerely care
about. Then we have a focus to inform our small and
large daily decisions.

*Today, I will think about my goals so that
I can be clearer about how to achieve them.*

*Prayer is less about changing the world
than it is about changing ourselves.*
— David J. Wolpe

Regardless of how we understand a Power greater than
ourselves, prayer is an important part of our lives. Relating to a Higher Power leads us out of our egotism into a
conscious relationship with powers far beyond ourselves.

How do we pray? We can use words to state what's
on our mind. We can say them silently or out loud. We
can quiet our mind and simply enter into the peace of
God, opening our mind to receive that deeper wisdom.
Drawing pictures can be a form of prayer. Playing music
or listening to music can be done prayerfully. This is not
so much a time to ask for special favors as a time to enter
the relationship and to receive the guidance that comes
from beyond our own power and conscious will.

*Today, I will quiet my mind for a few minutes
and enter consciously into a prayerful relationship
with my Higher Power.*

I not only bow to the inevitable;
I am fortified by it.
— *Thornton Wilder*

Some people understand great wisdom naturally without a struggle. Most of us have endured great pain and saw our lives careen out of control before we were willing to admit that we could be powerless. We wanted our pleasures and our escapes, and we did not want to conform to the truth. Our stories illustrate what happened when we refused to accept reality.

Now we also see how much stronger we become when we accept the wisdom of humility. When we put aside our hungry egos and bow to the inevitable truth, we begin to work with reality instead of against it. Our transformed lives are miracles because they grew from such out-of-control lives so filled with mistakes.

Today, I am grateful for the humility
and wisdom that has fortified me.

Man needs difficulties; they are
necessary for health.
— *Carl Jung*

When we are in the midst of problems and stresses, we can gather great strength from looking back at how far we have already come. True maturity gives us the perspective to see the bigger picture and to know that our present problems and distress will heal and pass into the background. At the same time, we can see from looking back that the obstacles we faced have changed us, and we have become stronger and better men as a result.

Today's obstacles, whether large or small, call us to bring our best wisdom in meeting them. We cannot foresee exactly how successful we will be. But we can resolve to be the best kind of man we know how to be, with honesty and gentleness. And that is a success we can guarantee.

Today, I will meet the obstacles I face
with all the maturity I've got and with
the strength of my honesty.

*When the mind is still . . . it returns to
itself, and by means of itself ascends to
the thought of God.*
— *Saint Basil the Great*

Our path is not leading us toward a physical place but toward the kind of person we are becoming. The Twelve Steps guide us to use daily meditation as a tool that helps us shape this new person. We take time for quiet moments, we still our thoughts, and in the stillness, without effort, our minds naturally open to introduce ourselves to ourselves. We become increasingly honest with ourselves, and some would say we hear the voice of God.

Daily readings can set a calming tone. Then we take a period of time, perhaps twenty minutes, for solitude undisturbed by others or by distracting phones or television. We find that when we set aside this quiet time, we actually seem to have more time, not less, for the other demands in our lives.

*Today, I will take a period of quiet time
to come back to myself.*

The pursuit of perfection often
impedes improvement.
— *George F. Will*

When we are haunted by feelings of shame or self-loathing, anything less than perfection can remind us of those feelings. We seek straight A's and when we succeed, we feel that it was only barely good enough. Sometimes we may even avoid trying something new because we refuse to make the necessary mistakes involved. In contrast, it is said that Persian rug weavers, in the course of creating their stunningly beautiful carpets, deliberately weave at least one mistake into every rug so as to not compete with God.

We could all take a lesson for our lives from those weavers. On a day when we are overcome by anxiety about making a mistake, we can be more relaxed and more effective if we start out deliberately intending to make at least one mistake before the day is over. That way, we can make a place for imperfection and go on from there to do our best and learn from the experience.

Today, I will make a place for imperfection
and learn from my mistakes.

Your pain is the breaking of the shell
that encloses your understanding.
— *Kahlil Gibran*

We seldom choose the pain that comes into our lives. Perhaps it comes as a consequence of other choices that we made. Perhaps it comes as a result of events that are no fault of our own. Either way, our suffering is something we have no choice about. But we do have choices about how we will respond to it. As men following a spiritual path, we have come to understand that whatever we have to deal with contains important lessons.

If a man falls and breaks his arm, no healing will come from blaming the rock he stumbled over or blaming the guy who put the rock in his way. He still must care for his broken bone, and the healing comes from within his own body.

We ask ourselves, "What am I to learn from this event? How can I take this experience and grow into a better, stronger man?" When we turn a painful thing into a way to grow, we turn a negative to our advantage, and our lives take a turn for the better.

Today, the pain I feel will point me
in a direction for my development.

*In running, it doesn't matter whether you
come in first, in the middle of the pack, or
last. You can say, "I have finished." There
is a lot of satisfaction in that.*

— *Fred Lebow*

In the ancient Greek competitions at Olympia, young
men came from all over the Greek nation to participate,
and great honor was bestowed on the winners. But just
to be a *participant*, in the Greek democratic mind, was a
high honor in itself.

We modern men sometimes lose that sense of true
honor. We think winning is the only goal. Such misguided beliefs are a distortion. Experience is much more
than winning, a lesson we can learn by watching athletes
with disabilities giving their all to their sport. These
athletes honor the true notion of participation.

*Today, I will participate with all of those
around me, to play, to run, and to work
for a better world.*

Sometimes I go about pitying myself,
and all the time
I am being carried on great winds across the sky.
— *Ojibwe song, translated by Frances Densmore,*
adapted by Robert Bly

Self-pity is a rather silly temptation. Our troubles may be very compelling and vivid. They may demand our attention. However, when we start to focus on ourselves rather than our challenges, we get distracted from coping with them. Self-pity is a form of self-centeredness. We think, "Why me?" or "Poor me," or "Look at all the suffering I endure." Whenever we let ourselves settle in on such self-focused thinking, we become smaller men.

One way to move out of such a dead end is to laugh at our narrowness. We can say, "There I go again, pitying myself when there are so many blessings in life." Another way out is to look at our challenges as teachers and open ourselves to learning their lessons.

Today, I will notice all the blessings that have
brought me this far in life and be open to the
lessons that are here for me to learn.

Love is presence.
— *Karolina Gerhardinger*

When we sit with a loved one who is very ill, we often feel helpless. When a friend is confronted with great pain or tragedy, we wonder, "What should I say?" To be comfortable in any relationship, we need to understand powerlessness and accept it. Sometimes the only and the most loving thing to do is to be present.

When we see our spouse or our partner make the same mistake over and over again, we want to take charge. When we don't get what we want from our beloved, we try to extract what we think we need. But we learn that true love exists within limits. We cannot fix others, and they cannot fix us. Once we accept the limits, once we accept powerlessness, we can relax into the love and enjoy its pleasures.

*Today, I will be present in the moment
with the people in my life.*

Everything I did in my life that was
worthwhile I caught hell for.
— *Earl Warren*

We have avoided conflict and sometimes taken the easier way when we should have stood up for what we believed in. We have procrastinated on difficult matters to keep the peace. Sometimes our fear of offending someone led us into dishonesty. We knew that if we said what we thought, or if we let others know our true feelings, we would have to deal with their reactions.

Great men do things that don't please everyone all the time. When we have true definition as a man, our boundaries will give others a target if they are looking for one. Perhaps, at work or at home, we have something we feel needs to be said, but we know it will displease others. Even our Twelve Step meetings take inventory on what is going well and what is not. So we learn to stand up for our beliefs and our principles. If no one ever gives us hell, we are probably not doing our best.

Today, I will act on my true beliefs
and express my honest feelings.

Success is how high you bounce
when you hit bottom.
— *General George S. Patton*

We all know about hitting bottom. Some of us look back and remember when we felt that we had lost everything. And some of us are grateful that we had a "high bottom." Either way, it is well for us to keep that memory close to us, because it is rich in lessons; hitting bottom motivated us to try something new. Our old patterns were broken, and we were opened to new ways of living.

When the future seemed most bleak, we were finally able to accept a better way. Little did we know that this very moment was the dawning of great prospects for our lives. We are grateful not for the crisis itself, but for its lessons and our current recovery. The bounce that follows hitting bottom continues for a lifetime as we continue to become better men.

Today, I am grateful for this path that leads out of
my deep valley and on to new vistas.

AUGUST

*Hope has nothing to do with optimism. Its opposite
is not pessimism but despair.*

— William Sloane Coffin

Despair is the loss of all hope. We are all vulnerable to
slipping into that frame of mind at times. When our
troubles are at their worst, we may indulge in angry and
rebellious negative thinking. Such negative thinking
is basically self-centered and self-indulgent. At other
times, we may feel that our lives are going well and that
we have no good reason to despair, yet we lose our spirit
and vitality.

We can use our spiritual focus at these times to interrupt the negative thoughts. When we catch ourselves
thinking life is unfair and we are worthless, we can stop
following our thoughts down that track. Simply turning
our attention elsewhere can help us restore our spirit for
life. This doesn't mean we fake optimism. It means we
choose to suspend our doubts and, just as we might try
on a new shirt, we try on the thought that we are in the
care of a Higher Power who accepts us as we are. When
we do that, a feeling of peace and calm will follow.

*Today, I will suspend feelings of despair and rest in the
faith that a Higher Power is present in my life.*

*I've always wanted to be somebody, but I see now
I should have been more specific.*

— *Lily Tomlin*

We are on an adult development journey. As we grow healthier, as we take our personal inventories, we develop into the kind of person we can respect and feel good about. From our addictive and codependent times, we know what it was like to feel empty—as if we were nobody. We had an exterior appearance of a whole person, but we were underdeveloped on the inside.

The promises of recovery always come true when we follow the steps toward honesty with ourselves and take responsibility for our actions. We may be assaulted by chaos and craziness around us, but this inner sense of self can never be taken away. And the longer we live in the light of the Twelve Steps and actively follow them, the more we develop this strong sense of self.

*Today, I will stay on the path because it guides
me toward greater development of my self.*

When the heart weeps because it has lost,
the spirit laughs because it has found.
— *Sufi mystic*

We must mourn our losses, and for some of us they are many. Whether we lost a loved one, or a marriage, or a job, mourning is necessary. Mourning is how we acknowledge that what we lost was dear to us and that we know it will change us. At the same time, we all know that good things can come from events we never would have chosen. Life does go on, and we can grow from our difficulties.

Our clearest example of that is seeing the good that can come from hitting bottom. After our addiction and codependency made us lose all that we could stand to lose, we surrendered to a spiritual program of recovery. Not everyone has to lose so much to gain a vibrant spiritual life. We didn't choose our losses. But for many of us, only after our losses mounted high enough were we opened up to grow spiritually.

Today, my spirit laughs because I am alive.

The name of this infinite and inexhaustible depth and ground of all being is God. That depth is what the word God means. And if that word has not much meaning for you, translate it, and speak to the depths of your life, of the source of your being, of your ultimate concern, of what you take seriously without any reservation.

— Paul Tillich

In the words of the Twelve Steps, we are guided toward God, as we understand God. Many of us are at first turned off by the word *God*. Some of us received early spiritual guidance through childhood religious training, but others had none at all—and some of us had negative experiences with organized religion. Now we are guided to grow into an adult form of spirituality. The words of today's quotation come from a great theologian who understood the same wisdom that the founders of Alcoholics Anonymous did. We don't have to limit our understanding of God by confining, dogmatic definitions. Our spiritual life is grounded in a sense of awe and rises from the deepest part of our being.

Today, my recovery is restored by God,
who surpasses all understanding.

Only your compassion and your loving kindness
are invincible, and without limit.
— *Thich Nhat Hanh*

We pray for the wisdom to distinguish between what we can change and what we cannot. This wisdom resides within our spiritual experience. This spiritual base is present even when our heart aches at the bedside of a loved one whose pain we cannot fix. We can be at peace in the wisdom of our hearts, knowing that the best we have to offer is our love and caring. We cannot do anything that will make a difference in taking away the pain, but just being there will make an immense difference.

We know that the spiritual truths that guide our lives are not based on the concrete world. Yet they light our paths. We see fear and terror in the world, yet we can find peace in knowing that our Higher Power will show us where to walk today. We cannot change the world today, but we can follow the light provided by the Twelve Steps. By doing our own small part, we offer a positive influence.

Today, as I live in the real world,
I will also live in the spiritual world.

Strive for continuous improvement
instead of perfection.
— *Kim Collins*

Doing our best is not perfection. We have goals and tasks before us. We work at them and we give them our best shot. That is all we need to do, and we deserve to feel all the self-respect any good man feels.

Some of our goals are big challenges. We can set aside any hopes of achieving them perfectly, but when we look back at what we have already done, we may remember that we have come further than we ever dreamed possible. If we expected perfection of ourselves, it would not help us. In fact, it would only get in the way of our work.

Today, I give my best to the work that is before me.
I will ask nothing more of myself.

I am always doing that which I cannot do,
in order that I may learn how to do it.
— *Pablo Picasso*

We fear trying something that we are not good at. We don't want to do something that we don't already have a handle on. If it isn't our usual way, we doubt that it's right for us. We are afraid of looking foolish, or we are suspicious of things that are unfamiliar.

But let us look at the most accomplished people we know. They didn't achieve greatness by repeating what they already knew. They felt strong enough within themselves—they had the courage—to take risks. Failures were part of their learning and became the basis for greater accomplishment.

Some men get older without ever getting wiser or more grown-up. They hold willfully on to what they already know. This lifestyle, living in the light of the Twelve Step program, challenges us to continually push into new territories of growth. We walk on paths where we cannot always see around the next turn. We don't know how to recover before we get on the path of recovery.

Today is another day in which I will do things
that push my learning forward.

The important thing in life is not to have
a good hand but to play it well.
— Louis N. Fortin

We all admire a man who gets dealt a difficult hand and plays it well. Most of us have been dealt a mixed hand in life. We had some bad breaks and some advantages. Many of those things we have no choice about; our starting point is the situation we find ourselves in. But we have a lot of choices about how we handle our situation. We cannot choose to have a lot of wealth today; we cannot choose to be free of family problems today; and if we have a health problem, that is what we must deal with. But we can choose how we will respond to our circumstances, and we can choose what kind of person we will be.

No one can take away the quality of our character or the attitude we have toward our situation. We find real meaning for life when we focus on the choices we can make. We set our sights on being the best kind of man we know how to be, even when we have to deal with tough circumstances.

Today, the meaning I get from life comes from
growing in my strength of character.

*Ritual is the way you carry the presence of the
sacred. Ritual is the spark that must not go out.*
— Christina Baldwin

We celebrate birthdays, anniversaries, births, gradua-
tions, and holidays. These events mark important times
and turning points. Many of us have not honored these
rituals, or we have doubted their meaning in life. Some
of us have seen rituals used in false and hollow ways,
and as a result deprived ourselves of the honest and deep
rewards that flow from true and meaningful observances.
Many of us are awakening from a time when all of life
lost its meaning, and rituals also seemed empty.

Now we are transforming into men who are not cynical, who don't diminish the landmarks in our lives. So we
send birthday cards, we light a candle for the memory of
a departed grandparent, and we give a gift to acknowledge our partner's special day. The ritual of observing
one month of sobriety can be even more meaningful
than one decade's observance. All events deserve some
attention to mark those times. They bring us to attention.
In our humility, we accept the attention, and we give
attention to others.

*Today, I will take note of important life events and
will plan to mark them with appropriate rituals.*

In every marriage more than a week old, there are grounds for divorce. The trick is to find, and continue to find, grounds for marriage.
— *Robert Anderson*

What is the purpose of a loving partnership? It is to enjoy the relationship. We reach adulthood with only the tools and expectations we learned as children about close relationships. Those childhood experiences, good or bad, are what we unconsciously play out unless we continue to develop. The intensity of adult love and passion can carry us into deep water, beyond our ability to trust, honor, and partner with someone. When we look at what we are asking from our partner, it is often the thing we would ask of the perfect parent.

Now it is time to become adult and carry our share. Rather than focus on what we want in a partner, we need to learn to be the best partner we can be. Each partner sets the standards for a good relationship. We cannot allow ourselves to say, "I only act this way because my partner acts that way." When we don't give that excuse, when we expect the best of ourselves regardless of our partner, we set the standard that we seek, and the relationship changes.

Today, I will be the best partner I can be, regardless of what my partner does.

Too often we enjoy the comfort of opinion
without the discomfort of thought.
— John F. Kennedy

Recovery from addiction and codependency goes beyond
the removal of the substance or the object of our obsession. Stopping our use is the necessary start to recovery.
But we can stop using and still continue the thoughts
and behavior that set us up for the disease. The biggest downfall for us all is our ego. We have a powerful
inner drive to get what we want. To justify our behavior, we may impulsively try to control our surroundings
and others. We say that a little bit of the old behavior
won't hurt anyone, or we are smarter than others, or
our behavior is only for the good of everyone. We have
to be fearless in our self-honesty. And, like dishonesty,
honesty builds on itself: one new self-admission leads
to another as we follow this spiritual path. We learn that
true humility actually arises from high self-esteem. We
learn to rely on our Higher Power to take care of us and
guide us. Our development as grown-up men continues
for our lifetime.

Today, I continue to be more honest
with myself than I used to be and continue
to behave in healthy ways.

God is like a mirror. The mirror never
changes, but everybody who looks at it
sees something different.
— *Rabbi Harold S. Kushner*

In their wisdom, the founders of Alcoholics Anonymous struggled with how to express the spirituality at the core of the program. They landed on the phrase "God *as we understood Him.*" That phrase is another way to express the idea of God as a mirror. Even those who try to define God will find that words cannot adequately describe the ultimate creator; instead, they place false limits on God.

When we face God, we don't see ourselves as we do in a mirror, but we see beyond ourselves. God provides us with a pathway out of our willful ego-based mind and expands our understanding as participants in the universe of creation. The awe and reverence and meaning of our spiritual lives call us to align ourselves with something far beyond our immediate pleasure and self-satisfying will.

Today, I am grateful for the spiritual awakening
that this program gives me.

*No one has completed his education who has
not learned to live with an insoluble problem.*
— *Edmund J. Kiefer*

Facing, for the first time, a stone wall that we cannot
change can be quite a shock. It's a huge emotional challenge that changes us from boys to men. Some people
first meet their insoluble problem in the form of the
death of a loved one, others through a child with an
incurable disability, and others by way of a chronic illness or an addiction. Whatever form a man's stone wall
takes, he naturally responds first with a refusal to accept
it and a search for a way around it. But when he ultimately learns to accept reality, he changes in a profound
way. He has stepped into the world of adults.

We used to feel that our addiction and codependency
were burdens, tragedies that we had to carry. But there is
a bright side to the dark stories of our past: when we got
honest about our powerlessness, we became real men.

*Today, I accept my powerlessness once again
and feel grateful for the wisdom it has taught me.*

Better to ask twice than to lose your way once.
— *Danish saying*

How many times have we heard that guys never want to stop and ask for directions? It is true that many of us would rather drive around searching for a place than stop and ask for help. Some of us say we enjoy solving the puzzle without asking for the answer. It's a trait that many men carry to extremes. We apply it to our lives with very serious consequences when we refuse to see a doctor for a medical condition, or we refuse to consult a therapist for personal problems, or we can't bring ourselves to go to a Twelve Step group.

Fortunately, we don't have to be permanently locked into those restrictions. We have now found the freedom and rich rewards that come from letting our guard down. The payoff for asking for help, and accepting it, has been far greater than the arrogance of doing everything without help.

Today, I will be open to all the help I can get.

A win in April is just as important as a win in September.
— Dave Bristol, Major League Baseball manager

Hitting bottom and turning to recovery is an important part of our life story. Many of us lost almost everything before we started to recover. Others had the good fortune to get into recovery early, while most parts of our lives were still intact. Some of us relapsed and had to hit bottom more than once. But once we are on the path of recovery, those distinctions make no difference. Nobody is more or less a codependent or an addict. Nobody is immune from the destruction that our old ways would bring if we returned to them.

A high bottom is like a win in April. It doesn't count any less in the long run. It doesn't make us any less an addict or any less codependent, and it doesn't mean that we have any more control than any of our fellow recovering friends. We are all just one bad decision away from reactivating our old ways. The only important distinction is that we are on the path now.

Today, I am grateful to be sober and in recovery,
following this path of a better life.

*The great man is he who does not
lose his child-heart.*

— *Mencius*

No matter what we have done or what has happened
to us, no matter how guilty, worried, or fearful we feel,
there was a time when we were small, innocent, and
openhearted toward the world. That happy and playful
boy still lives within us. Sometimes he seems like a distant memory, but we would do well to bring him close
to us, give him a place in our awareness, and honor and
protect him.

Some of us remembered that little boy being treated
too harshly or shamed too deeply, and we adopted false
attitudes of disgust toward him. But we can go back still
further to a time when he was innocent and we could
love him. A strong and healthy man carries that boy close
to his heart and lets him come forth to be playful and
lighthearted. That boy can be the source of eagerness
to learn and hope for the future. He can put himself in
the shoes of the small and the weak and treat them with
gentleness.

*Today, my child-heart beats within me
as strongly as it ever did.*

Marriage is our last best chance to grow up.
— *Joseph Barth*

Most of us think of marriage in romantic terms. We imagine finding the "right one," and we form a vision of the ideal mate. Others of us have given up on ever finding a lifelong partner. The romance of a relationship naturally plays a less important role as we deal with practical matters like house cleaning, earning a living, and child care. When problems develop, we think about how we want our partner to change. If only they would listen to us more. If only they would spend money more responsibly. If only . . . If only . . . Most of our ideas about improving our marriage are left over from child-hood ideas about how we would like to be taken care of. We want more attention. We want more love. We want to change our partners to satisfy our needs better. But when we give up on changing our partners, we grow up ourselves. When we accept that our partners are also on a life path, which is not identical to our own, we can accept them as friends, and the good things we share grow in importance.

Today, I will be a full-grown man, responsible
for my part in my intimate relationship,
and let the rest go.

*Facing our pain, seeing the enemy as a potential
ally, learning to wait, giving inner events time to
ripen and mature—are methods we can use . . .
for transformation.*
— Harry R. Moody and David Carroll

Sometimes we need to break out of our established ways
of thinking. We need to do what is counterintuitive in
order to solve a problem. This program is a path of personal transformation. We lay the cornerstones for this
transformation by trying something different. Instead
of forcing change, we get out of the way for change to
happen.

We are not being passive. We are actively engaging
in a new way. Who or what are my enemies? What am
I battling? What if I look at enemies as potential allies
who could teach me something? What if I didn't work
so hard at fixing a loved one's problems? What if I decide
to see where it leads?

Transformation creates new outcomes. As we try them
on, we are transformed.

*Today, I will be open to seeing things in a new way.
I will assume that I don't understand things completely
and that I can still learn more.*

Strength and tolerance are partners.
— *Kahlil Gibran*

We admire strength. As boys we looked up to the raw strength and power we saw in the biceps of big men and older boys. We tested our muscles and those of our pals. We worked at our own physical power to gain the respect of others.

As grown men our admiration has grown up with us. Now we have a much bigger understanding of strength. We know that most strength can't be measured in the size of our muscles. The strongest men are often the kindest and gentlest toward those around them. And often those who are most unsure of their strength try to steal power from others by intimidation, ridicule, and displays of force.

A man stands tallest when he shows tolerance toward those who are different from him and those who are not popular with others. Some say that it builds strength to stand up for others who are vulnerable.

Today, I will show tolerance for those who are different or more vulnerable than I am.

*To be tested is good. The challenged life
may be the best therapist.*
— *Gail Sheehy*

We don't learn anything new from successfully doing
things that we have already mastered. We learn from our
mistakes and the obstacles that appear in our path. They
call on us to come up with new skills. We have certainly
come to this path after facing plenty of challenges. And
we know that a problem doesn't guarantee that growth
will be the outcome.

A problem or a challenge can simply be a net loss until
we turn it into an opportunity for growth. If we make
a mistake and simply feel stuck in shame and regret, it
leads to nothing more. But if we have an element of faith,
we can look for its message. That is the path to greater
strength and maturity.

*Today, I will notice my mistakes
and use them to grow.*

Good thoughts bear good fruit, bad thoughts bear
bad fruit—and man is his own gardener.
— *James Allen*

Before we entered our program of healing and recovery, we didn't recognize our thinking patterns as addictive and codependent. We simply thought our thoughts. Our attitudes seemed natural to us. Now we have learned from looking back that we had many self-serving and distorted ways of seeing life. Because of our need for control and our dependence on addictive ways, we had very nearsighted vision. Many of us indulged in a cynical and dark view of life. We used and controlled others to achieve our needs, and we were often ruled by fear.

Now we are learning that we can cultivate a healthier and happier state of mind. We need not be constantly vigilant about our safety and comfort. We have friends who are genuine and trustworthy. We can rest assured that our Higher Power will always be with us. We are created to be on this earth, and we have a right to take a place among the rest of humankind.

Today, I am grateful for a healthy state of mind.

*Experience is not what happens to a man. It is
what a man does with what happens to him.*
— *Aldous Huxley*

What does it take for a man to be called *experienced*?
Whom do we turn to when we look for someone who
knows the ropes? We aren't likely to seek out someone
who remains in the midst of his chaos. But if a man has
been there and learned from his experience, he stands
taller than everyone else. He is a kind of hero with much
to teach us.

Most of us have plenty of experience. But how can we
learn from our experience? We need to stop, take time
to reflect, and be honest with ourselves. When we don't
take time to slow down, we cannot learn from our wealth
of experience. We only pile one event on another and
run from one demand to another. We can change that
by adding time for reflection and contemplation to our
schedule. A day off with no demands is valuable for the
soul. A retreat to a quiet place, time for fishing, or golf,
or hiking is not self-indulgence when we understand
that we are on a spiritual path. Twenty minutes of quiet
every day for solitude and reflection makes us wiser,
stronger men for the lives we are leading.

*Today, I will take time to reflect, to be honest with myself,
and to absorb the lessons of my experiences.*

When I found out I thought God was white,
and a man, I lost interest.

— *Alice Walker*

On our path, spiritual development and renewal is constant. We make time for conscious contact with God as we understand God, and our understanding keeps forming. Our childhood images of God may be too limited. That doesn't mean we have to toss out the whole concept, but our understanding has to grow up with us.

To some, God is the spirit and the feeling of camaraderie in shared fellowship. To some, God is the God expressed in their traditional religion. Others say that God is simply beyond all definition, an ultimate that exceeds our rational mind. Others say God is the sense we have that we are never alone. And to some, God is found in the beauty of nature. This program of healing and recovery guides us to make a decision to turn our life and our will over to the God of our understanding. And we can expect that as the relationship grows so will our understanding.

Today, I am grateful for the presence
of God as I carry on with my life.

*Storytelling is giving shape to the
amorphous chaos of life.*
—*Anonymous*

When we put words to what has happened to us, we can begin to learn from our experience. We carry images within us that are the building blocks of our stories, but we only begin to make sense of them when we put them into words. Talking with a trusted friend, or speaking in a meeting, or telling a therapist about our experiences gives them a shape. The words give us a way to understand, and they build a bridge to others. We may feel deeply alone if we keep our memories and images to ourselves. When we begin to talk, as we tell our story, we learn from our own words, and they take us deeper into our truth.

We don't tell our story only once. We do it over and over again. It brings relief from the traumas and releases us from the prison of our past. Each time we talk, even recounting the same events, we are somewhat different because we have grown, and we see our own story from a new perspective. Listening to other men's stories and telling our own is one of the special tools for spiritual growth that we use on this recovery path.

*Today, I will talk to someone about
an experience or a feeling.*

Noble deeds and hot baths are
the best cures for depression.
— Dodie Smith

When we change our lives, we give up old patterns. Some of these old patterns, as harmful as they may have been, were like our best friends. We could turn to them for comfort and escape. After giving them up, and after the first elated feelings of liberation, we may also have to deal with the depression and grief of loss. What should we remember at these times? First, the loss of energy, the dark mood, the hopelessness—all will pass, and we will regain our vitality and joy of life. Second, it helps to stay active. Physical activity is one of the best medicines for a depressed mood: vigorous walks, physical labor, or a good workout at the gym. Another kind of activity is helping others, reaching out to those in need of companionship and a helping hand. It is surprising how good it feels to make a difference in another person's life. The third thing we can do is stop our negative thoughts. We can simply interrupt a train of thought in the same way we might interrupt a conversation and change the subject. Finally, we can take comfort in the faith that our Higher Power will provide what we need in the long run.

Today, I will take good care of my mental well-being.

Smooth seas do not make skillful sailors.
— *African proverb*

Only by meeting many different conditions and being challenged by problems do we develop great skill in dealing with life. We say a man is soft who has always had everything handed to him. We admire a man who has met great challenges and come through them. However, while we are struggling and when the challenges are really on top of us, we may not feel that we are in the midst of some admirable battle. We are more likely to simply feel burdened and stressed, not knowing what the outcome will be.

When the sailor is in the midst of the storm, he focuses intently on what he has to do right now. He learns to read the wind and the waves in these extreme conditions by being there and by learning from others who are more experienced. That is a model for developing our skills on this sea of life.

*Today, I will focus on what I need to do
just for today, and I will learn from those
who are more experienced than I am.*

The wise person questions himself,
the fool others.

— *Henri Arnold*

We pray for wisdom, and sometimes we achieve it. The strongest and wisest of men are not threatened by questioning their own answers. If we draw conclusions and blindly stick to them, we can never learn anything new. We have often made the mistake of avoiding the appearance of ignorance. Instead, we are at our best when we give ourselves the privilege of being a learner. When someone tells us something we don't understand or agree with, our best response is to ask for more information. We can take our ego out of the equation, surrender our need to be right, and simply try to learn what is being told to us. What is it that I don't understand here? What does the other person see that I am missing? When we attain a moment of wisdom, we are open to learning.

Today, I will give myself the privilege of being a learner.

The creative process is a process
of surrender, not control.
— *Julia Cameron*

When creative artists describe the experience of creating a painting or writing a novel, they often talk about feeling that they are given inspiration, as if it comes from outside them. They tell us that if they are too willful or too deliberate, they get in the way.

When we begin to walk the Twelve Steps, we enter that same kind of process. We are led to surrender—not in defeat, but to let ourselves be cared for. As men we may know little about becoming so vulnerable. Many of us concluded long ago that vulnerability only led to pain and defeat. Perhaps we could let a lover care for us, especially in an erotic or sexual way. But opening ourselves to the care of our group, our sponsor, or our Higher Power was outside anything we had ever tried. On this path, our whole life is a creative process. We can't know exactly where it will take us. That is the adventure—and it is infinitely long. We continue the creative way, daily learning new things and developing new experiences. We are present and open, and we know the feeling of being spiritually awake.

Today, my life will be a creative adventure.

God provides minimum protection,
maximum support.
— *William Sloane Coffin*

People often ask how a just God could allow innocent children to starve to death, or how an all-powerful God could send devastating storms that cause pain and destruction across the land. Great theologians tell us that we cannot hold God responsible for the evil and pain in the world. Bad things happen, and they aren't the work of God. In a random universe, God's design is to be present with us and support us through the troubles we face.

When we turn our life and will over to the care of God, we can't expect God to bring us special magical favors. Instead, we turn over our willfulness and childish demanding nature to God who helps us be strong, maintain our spirit, and continue on our path. Then God never leaves us alone, even when we defy God, even when we make bad choices. God is there loving us, even when we feel worthless.

Today, I will open myself to the
support of my Higher Power.

It's just human. We all have the jungle inside us. We all have wants and needs and desires, strange as they may seem.
— Diane Frolov and Andrew Schneider,
Northern Exposure

Sex is a driving force in our lives. Many of us in recovery find that our sexuality is another part of our lives that is changing. Some of us suddenly find we can't perform in sobriety as we did while we were using. Others of us are recovering from addiction to sexual behaviors. When we are facing difficulty with our sexuality, it is sometimes hard to think of it as a source of pleasure and reward.

In fact, our sexuality can recover and heal, just as any other aspect of our personality can recover. Grown-up, adult sex is more comfortable, more sensuous, and more fulfilling than adolescent sex. That is only possible when we are sober and awake to our lives. Many of us need to start by tuning in to our bodies and the sensations we experience now in our sobriety. Along with that, we may need to embrace the fact that we deserve to have sexual pleasure, not as something we are owed, but as something we can seek and indulge in. These changes happen gradually over time as recovery progresses.

Today, I am grateful for the energizing force of sex and passion in my life.

Solitude is the furnace of transformation.
— *Henri Nouwen*

In solitude, we quietly unwrap the honesty that is deep within us. Sitting in the company of just ourselves and God, we gradually realize that no one else is observing us and the image we present. Solitude may throw us into some confusion at first, or some discomfort. We might feel pushed to escape, to get out of there into a place with some action and distractions. Transformation is frightening because it is a process that we do not fully control. We can block it, or stop it, but if we allow it to progress, it is controlled by our deeper honesty and by the spirit of a Higher Power.

We can make a simple decision that we will enter the experience of solitude. We can do that for a few minutes every day in a special place we set aside, or we can set aside several days of retreat. However, we cannot create our own transformation by a simple decision. Our solitude prepares us and softens the guards we have set against the frightening process of transformation. And as we are ready, change and growth arrive.

Today, I will open myself through
moments of solitude.

SEPTEMBER

I have a great deal more respect for someone who keeps coming back after losing heartbreaker after heartbreaker than I do for the winner who has everything going for him.

— Wilt Chamberlain

One aspect of recovery is dealing with relapse. After we have been in recovery and then fall back into our addiction or codependent behaviors, we are filled with regret. We may also be stricken with strong feelings of shame and a defeatist attitude. But if we come back to our meetings and get back in the program, we deserve only self-respect. We are not defeated unless we give up on ourselves.

No bad experience is a total loss unless we refuse to learn something from it. Recovery from relapse begins when we relearn that we are powerless over our addiction. It calls for us to make something positive out of the negative experience. We examine the point where we resumed our addictive and codependent thinking, even before we realized it. Experienced people in the program know that we learn to prevent relapse by returning to recovery after we have fallen away.

Today, I have the greatest respect for those who keep coming back.

It is with our passions as with fire and water:
they make good servants but bad masters.

—Aesop

Our passions—whether they be sex, anger, love, or an intense interest in a hobby—are energizing and enriching dimensions of our lives. On the other hand, who hasn't made mistakes with his passions? Who hasn't had regrets about his actions when a drive became a master rather than a servant? Some of us are recovering from problems with anger or sex. Many of us are subject, in our recovery, to overinvolvement with some new passion, such as work or a game or a hobby, that once again takes us away from our relationships and our peace of mind.

A man grows up by making mistakes and learning from them. We learn to steer a car by turning the wheel, overcorrecting, and recorrecting. It is when we refuse to acknowledge that our passion has become our master that we cannot make the needed adjustments to keep our passions in balance. Keeping an honest, unflinching personal inventory is what a strong man does.

Today, I am grateful for the passions
that serve my well-being.

Our faith should quell our fears,
never our courage.
— *William Sloane Coffin*

Courage is a core value for a man, but without fear, there is no need for courage. Our path to this point in our lives was governed by fear more than most of us ever realized or wanted to admit. We were driven into the arms of addiction and codependency by fear and anxiety. Our substance of choice gave us a feeling of control, and we developed a knee-jerk habit of grasping for it. Even before our fears for our well-being could rise to consciousness, we were scanning the world for ways to gain that sense of control. For some of us that meant anxiously controlling the people around us; for others it meant escaping into gaming, gambling, or pornography.

The centerpiece of our recovery is a completely different way to soothe our uneasiness. It is a belief that if we turn to a Higher Power, we can quell our fears and find serenity without the destructiveness of our old habits. We learned the old ways over time, and this new way takes time to learn as well. We can start immediately to turn our life over to a Higher Power, and as we do, we will find greater comfort in return.

Today, I will admit my fears and anxieties, finding
courage by turning to faith in a Higher Power.

*If people concentrated on the really
important things in life, there'd be
a shortage of fishing poles.*
— Doug Larson

We win admiration for work, achievement, and competitiveness. We are told that a good man is a good provider. These are external rewards, but the rewards of relaxing, of rest and quiet solitude, of recreation are not external. We feel those rewards internally. They are the rewards of personal growth. Work addiction is a tempting mistake for us recovering men. We had big problems in the past, and it feels wonderful to know that we can be competent in our work. We lived in crisis, and our lives were out of control. That memory can haunt us for a lifetime, so work may now provide a welcome structure. But too much work can be another distraction from the important things.

Sometimes we may need to schedule some free time with our families and with our friends, time simply for loafing. Taking a half hour each day for quiet thought and reflection, with no external sign of accomplishment, helps us to become better men.

*Today, I will lighten my focus on work
and make time for play.*

Nothing happens unless first a dream.
— *Carl Sandburg*

Knowing ourselves is partly a matter of forming our dreams for who we want to become. These dreams are constantly evolving as long as we live. They give us purpose in our daily lives and point us in the direction we want to go. We can advance our growth by simply writing down a few of our dreams and goals. We can keep this list with us, on our phone or in our billfold, and we can reflect on it, use it to guide our actions, and modify it over time.

Sometimes we resist writing these things down, or even thinking about them, because we may not dare to admit our true motivations and dreams. But even if we don't admit our dreams, they still shape our behavior. When we acknowledge what we most want, we become better men.

*Today, I will take the risk to form
a clear idea of my fondest dreams.*

*Never bear more than one kind of trouble
at a time. Some people bear all three—
all they have had, all they have now, and
all they expect to have.*
— *Edward Everett Hale*

Learning to manage our worries and our darker memories is part of becoming a stronger person. If we don't exercise some choice over them, we can get swallowed up in a chain reaction: one problem ignites fear and pain about all the others. Understanding the wisdom of powerlessness becomes an excellent guide for us in focusing our mind when troubles assail us.

We accept that many things aren't within our control to create or to stop. All we can do is hope and pray and turn the results over to our Higher Power. We don't subject ourselves to a pity session or a major anxiety attack by letting one challenge remind us of everything that has gone wrong in the past or could go wrong tomorrow. We live in the present, we deal with what is before us at the moment, and we pray for the serenity to accept the rest.

Today, I will live in the present.

You never really understand a person until
you consider things from his point of view.
— *Harper Lee*

We came to this spiritual path with habits and addictions that had trapped us in a very childish and self-centered mind. Our strong need for control, our sense that we could count only on ourselves, blocked us from learning to understand others. Now we are finding a fellowship in which we don't have to be alone. Others reach out to us in helpful and generous ways. We have friends.

The wonderful thing about a good friend is that we gain the opportunity to see through someone else's eyes. We can borrow this person's life experiences as if they were our own and learn those lessons without making the same mistakes. Or we can borrow our friend's feeling of hope when our own hope is flagging. It's not necessary to agree with someone to see things from his point of view. Sometimes we simply enlarge our scope by saying, "I see why you could feel that way." The fellowship of good friends is one of the most humanizing experiences we can have.

Today, I will listen to others and
try to borrow their eyes and ears.

Learn the alchemy true human beings know:
The moment you accept what troubles you've
been given, the door will open.

— *Rumi*

Step One requires us to admit the trouble we face. We now know that until we do that, no progress can be made. Some of us honestly didn't see the true nature of our powerlessness. Others knew the truth but refused to admit it openly. Once we have faced up to such a big admission of powerlessness, we start to see an important pattern. Now we can apply it to many everyday situations. Owning up to the truth of a problem opens the door. Something changes, and we begin to deal with problems in a new and more effective way.

Whether we have diabetes that needs daily attention, or a child with special needs, or a work situation that never improves, the formula is the same. Accept the matter for what it is, as hard as that may be, and new answers begin to emerge. In part, this is a spiritual process that seems to naturally lead us to the next step of turning to our Higher Power for comfort and guidance. This readies us for new possibilities.

Today, I will try to accept the reality that I face,
so that I am ready for new answers.

*Anyone who keeps the ability
to see beauty never grows old.*
— *Franz Kafka*

We ask ourselves, "What really counts when everything else is stripped away? What do we still value?" Beauty is one of those values for many of us. It might be the beauty of the outdoors, solitude in the wilderness, a symphony, a special painting, or the athletic grace of a pitcher as he hurls the baseball across home plate. Something stirs within us when we see beauty. Many would call that a spiritual experience because it seems to touch the soul of our being.

We can feel vulnerable when we have such experiences, and some of us have learned to run roughshod over those moments. We smother that part of our soul so that we don't have to feel our manhood threatened. Now we are learning new lessons. We are growing into stronger, more open, and more spiritual men. Beauty, wherever we see it, is part of our spiritual life.

*Today, I am open to the stirring
in my soul when I see beauty.*

*There are no secrets to success. It is
the result of preparation, hard work,
learning from failure.*

— *Colin Powell*

Preparation consists of becoming entirely ready. On this path, where we have faced the ultimate truth of power-lessness, we accept the deep wisdom of adulthood: some things cannot be changed by the force of our will. So our work is to make ourselves ready for change to come to us. We work on our willfulness, our moral character, our honesty, and our openness to the spiritual presence. Readiness means that when opportunities for change appear, we accept them. It means that change comes as a gift, not of our own invention. As our relationship with ourself grows, our relationships with others improve. As our relationship with our Higher Power grows, the cravings that we could not subdue by force of will are simply and quietly lifted. It is a spiritual paradox: this is not a passive path we are walking; it requires hard work. And yet the success we find is a gift that comes to us, and we can only accept it.

*Today, I will continue to work, making myself
ever more ready to receive the gifts of the spirit.*

I don't have to be what you want me to be.
— *Muhammad Ali*

We only truly become ourselves from the inside out. During our active addiction, many of us tried so hard to please others that we lost any sense of who we were, or we created an external image that would get others to like us. Some of us lost ourselves in codependently taking care of others. So much focus on others never led us to know ourselves or truly develop our interior private self.

This program, with its twelve suggested Steps, is really a road map for the formation of a true self. At the beginning, we may feel empty inside, as if hardly any self exists. But at least some small, undeveloped self is always there, and it will grow. By taking inventory of ourselves, by becoming accountable for our actions, and by developing our spirituality, we become truly whole.

Today, I will be the person I know from inside myself and not try to create an image to please others.

Abuse is something that is done to us.
It is not who we are.
— Euan Bear and Peter Dimock

Everyone has some experience with being treated badly. Sometimes that experience leaves us with scars that affect us for years. Abuse means we feel overwhelmed by someone's power to hurt us or use us. It steals our basic human dignity. Afterward we feel belittled, as if something basic about us is missing or blemished.

Recovery means we restore our feeling of personal dignity. To begin that part of our recovery, we first name the abuse. Someone beat us up, someone called us names, or someone used our body for his or her own pleasure. Abuse may even come from someone we love and trust. After we name the abuse, we tell a trusted friend what happened. In this process, we start the work of placing those experiences outside of ourselves instead of holding them deep inside where they confuse us. Ultimately, our recovery frees us.

Today, I understand that even though bad
things happened to me, I am basically good,
just like everyone else.

You can learn little from victory. You can learn
everything from defeat.

— Christy Mathewson

We all know the face of painful defeat. We tried to win, but some of our ways led to disgrace and shame. We used unwise and self-indulgent methods to cope with life's problems. Those defeats were devastating. But it's not only bad choices and mistakes that create loss and heartache. Inevitably, adult life forces everyone to face powerlessness. That is a spiritual lesson that some of us accept more readily than others. Some guys don't easily give up the heady feeling of power and the pride of doing things their own way, even when their own way brings repeated defeat.

With only victories, we might stay stuck as superficial boys for the rest of our lives. What would push us to learn? From the broken pieces of painful events, we are forced to learn something new. We can no longer hold on to our voracious appetites and our stubborn willfulness. We have to finally open our minds to the wisdom of others. Through our failures we are strengthened. In facing powerlessness, we truly grow from boyishness into genuine manhood.

> *Today, I am grateful for all that*
> *I have learned from my defeats.*

I began to have an idea of my life, not as the slow shaping of achievement to fit my preconceived purposes, but as the gradual discovery and growth of a purpose which I did not know.
— Joanna Field

When we pledge to turn our life and our will over to the care of God, we have taken a profound step. With those words, we enter into the mystery of the spiritual life. We move from feeling alone to trusting that our Higher Power will guide our choices. We move from focusing on what we want to focusing on who we will become. We stop trying to control everything and become open to the mystery that underlies life.

For some of us, today presents challenges and worries. Some of us are anxious about a problem at work or within our family. We may have a painful dispute with our life partner. In the wisdom of the spiritual path, we can lean back on the faith that we don't have to deal with these things alone. We can do what is possible, and we can rely on the care of God to work in the ways of God.

Today, I am grateful for the care and purposes of God to lead me in dealing with life.

*It's not true that nice guys finish last. Nice guys
are winners before the game even starts.*
— Addison Walker

Being considerate, civil, generous, and interested in
others forms the basis of good character and good relationships with others. When we stop being so focused
on ourselves, when we stop trying to come out ahead of
everyone else, our world opens up. We suddenly have
good, supportive friendships that are more valuable than
material winnings.

The Golden Rule is ancient advice that is expressed in
many languages and world religions. It says, "Do unto
others as you would have them do unto you." It is a small
man who takes away someone else's power to advance
his own. A strong man can confidently cheer for the
strength of others.

Today, I am grateful for the good friends in my life.

> *If stupidity got us into this mess,*
> *then why can't it get us out?*
> — *Will Rogers*

When we are in the midst of our worst problems, we often behave stubbornly, trying harder to gain control of what is out of control. Because we feel alone, or because we insist on doing things our own way, we repeatedly apply the same solutions that repeatedly produce the same problems. We forget that as human beings we require the help of others to live happy and healthy lives. We need all the help we can get. Without the input and wisdom of others, we are stuck with our limited or mistaken ideas.

Perhaps today we are faced with problems that have no clear solutions. We can't see an obvious way around them, and we can't see a new answer. The sooner we accept our true nature and bring others into our questions, the sooner we will be able to consider new ideas and take in the wisdom of our friends.

> *Today, I resolve to talk to my friends*
> *about what is weighing on my mind.*

If a man does his best, what else is there?
— *General George S. Patton*

For many of us, competition is so ingrained that we have a knee-jerk competitive reaction to almost every encounter with another man. Competition is great fun among friends. Testing our skill, our power, and our wits against others helps us know ourselves better and shows us what we are capable of. It is a kind of closeness among friends to playfully compete. But when competition becomes our only way to relate to others, it keeps people away. When we can only respond with a wisecrack or a one-up comment, we are just a one-trick pony, reacting out of weakness and fear of getting close.

Among true and trusted friends, a man is entitled to show more than his strength and his guarded side. A true friend doesn't use our vulnerability or our mistakes to take advantage of us. When he holds them as a trust that he guards and protects, he shows the mark of true friendship.

Today, I will be the best person that I can be,
and that includes honesty about my weaknesses
and vulnerability.

There is no saint without a past—
no sinner without a future.
— *Saint Augustine*

How can we not believe in redemption when we see it demonstrated all around the room every time we attend a meeting? Our most respected members were once in crisis at the bottom of their lives. And when we contemplate our own feelings of guilt and shame, we need humility to accept the fact that we, too, can be restored. All saints and all sinners reflect the same truth: all human beings are imperfect. If we are truly humble, we can accept our humanity, stop expecting perfection, and forgive our mistakes.

We take our personal inventory and assume responsibility for our actions because that process starts to release us from guilt and shame. The most dignified man is not the guy who never made a mistake, but the one who faced his mistakes and went forward living a better life.

Today, I am grateful for the redemption
this program leads me toward.

Man must search for what is right,
and let happiness come on its own.
— *Johann Pestalozzi*

We make a mistake when we try to pursue happiness as if it were something we could achieve and hold. Happiness comes and goes. It is a by-product. If we seek to become better men, to fulfill our deeper values, happiness will visit us along the way. On the other hand, to seek happiness as a goal and expect to hold on to it will only bring frustration and self-pity.

Our human nature calls us to have goals and values that transcend the limits of our own selves. We feel deep love for our children, and we want to be the best father possible. When we fulfill that goal, we feel happy. We have a great love for music or art, and we want to participate in it by creating it or appreciating it. When we fulfill that desire, we feel happy. Hard work is not often thought of as happiness, but its outcome often brings happiness.

Today, I am working for goals that I believe in.
Happiness will come and go along the way.

Prayer is not asking. It is a longing of the soul.
It is daily admission of one's weakness.
— *Mahatma Gandhi*

We got into our difficulties because of the ways we managed our desires and longings. When we found ways to easily cool our pain or satisfy our longings, we got hooked on them. After we learned that our controlling and addictive behaviors could make us feel comfortable and bring intense pleasure, we got even more hooked on them. But they quickly proved to be false answers.

Now we are a bit wiser, and we strive to avoid those alluring pitfalls. So we daily turn in prayer to our Higher Power. This is the longer, slower approach to managing our desires and longings. Ultimately, what we sought in the easy answers was something deeper, more satisfying. Through our spiritual life, we find satisfaction to our longings and yearnings.

Today, I bring my powerlessness to a
Higher Power for care and guidance.

For man, autumn is a time of harvest,
of gathering together. For nature, it is
a time of sowing, of scattering abroad.
— *Edwin Way Teale*

Autumn is a good metaphor for the Twelfth Step. In this Step, we are reaping the benefits of recovery, but it is also important for continued recovery that we spread the word. It is a time to tell our stories and invite others to have what we have found. Nature sustains itself not by hoarding and keeping its bounty locked up, but by generously and prolifically scattering its seeds to the wind. We need to do the same in recovery.

The early recoverers who discovered the path that became the Twelve Steps quickly recognized that their own precarious progress required them to tell their stories to other alcoholics. They asked permission from other suffering addicts to be allowed to tell their stories, not to promote their method, but to sustain their own progress. We, too, need to tell other people where we have been and what we have found.

Today, I will be generous in giving away
what I have learned.

Character consists of what you do
on the third and fourth tries.
— *James A. Michener*

With the Serenity Prayer, we seek to accept the things we cannot change and to change the things we can. Many of us have been discouraged by repeated relapses and by overwhelming problems. This is a time when we need to discern between what we can and cannot change. A man with diabetes, after first losing his eyesight and then one leg to his disease, says that he carries on, loving life, because he still chooses to have purpose and meaning. He cannot change his disease; he has to accept it.

Our heroes aren't the guys who had it easy. The greatest heroes are always the ones who battled with discouragement and great challenges. A relapse isn't the end of the story. We have risked losing everything, including our lives, but if we survived, we never go back to square one. Our past, no matter how dark, is a resource to build on. If we have relapsed, we don't lose what we learned in our past time of recovery. We only need to diligently learn from our mistakes and return to what we know recovery still offers.

Today, I resolve to never give up on life.

*To be sensual is to respect and rejoice in
the force of life itself, and to be present in
all that one does, from the effort of loving
to the breaking of bread.*

— Phyl Garland

Sensuality and sexuality are very spiritual experiences.
When we take pleasure in our senses and take joy in life,
we reach into the spiritual realm. We enter that realm
when we are present in the moment, drinking in the
warmth of the bright sunshine, smelling the freshness of
the air, savoring the aroma of our toast in the morning,
relishing good music, or indulging in the good feelings
of touch and gentle eye contact.

Of course, this sensual side can be distorted. Many of
us have been so taken with sensuality that we got lost in
it. We corrupted our spirituality with bad judgment or
abusive behaviors. Now we are growing into good men
who love life and respect the wonders of sex and sensuality. We are learning to be present to all sensations, to
the very force of life as we experience it, and as adults,
we are wisely choosing when to indulge in them heartily.

*Today, I celebrate all my senses and
seek a happy, healthy sexuality.*

The remarkable thing is that we really love our neighbor as ourselves: we do unto others as we do unto ourselves. We hate others when we hate ourselves. We are tolerant toward others when we tolerate ourselves. We forgive others when we forgive ourselves. We are prone to sacrifice others when we are ready to sacrifice ourselves.

— *Eric Hoffer*

Our healing begins within ourselves. We may have deep feelings of low self-esteem. We didn't grow up believing that we were good. We may carry feelings of guilt for bad choices we made. We may not expect to be loved, and when the love is there, we may not see it for what it is.

That is where we must start our recovery. We must treat ourselves with respect, forgive our wrongs, and accept forgiveness. A good man with strong self-esteem doesn't think he is without fault or superior to others. He knows that he is a mixture of many qualities, good and bad, as all people are. He doesn't attack his own nature by calling himself stupid. When we learn to treat ourselves with the respect that our creator has for us, our love and respect are reflected in all of our relationships.

Today, I pledge to be respectful and forgiving toward myself.

No one can begin to feel better about oneself
until brutal self-honesty prevails.
— *Donna Thompson*

We have sometimes used words to fool ourselves and fool others. We say "I'll try" when we really don't want to face a challenge. Or we say "I'll think about that" when we simply want to avoid talking about something.

Some challenges in life require action. Nothing less will do. Do we say that we will "try" to call our sponsor, or do we call him? Do we "try" to work on a Step for our recovery, or do we work on it? When someone gives us a word of wisdom that we don't want to hear, do we engage with him, perhaps even tell him it's hard for us to hear, or do we say "I'll think about that" just to get him off our back?

Today, I will not fool myself.
I will use words that admit my truth.

The Lord created me at the beginning of his work, the first of his acts of long ago.
— *Proverbs 8:22*

All of God's creation deserves respect. Many of us have felt that we were bad or worthless, or beyond the reach of genuine acceptance. If we believed in God, perhaps we thought we deserved God's condemnation more than we deserved grace. Today, we are reminded that we are part of creation. God is everywhere in creation and within us.

Certainly, some of our actions were wrong. Certainly, we must be accountable for our bad deeds. But what we do is not who we are. Our deeds are not our spirit. At the core, we are sacred creatures of God. Being accountable is a high and noble thing, and it is one way that we pay respect to ourselves and our God.

Today, I will respect myself as part of God's work.

The heart forms itself according to what it loves.
— *Karolina Gerhardinger*

All great spiritual traditions speak to us about our desires and how we manage them. Their universal wisdom tells us that our handling of our yearnings and attachments affects the kind of person we become. For us addicts and codependents, this has special meaning. We may have fallen in love with alcohol, or another drug, or another behavior. As codependents, we also become so committed to the care and control of others that we never develop our own spirit. People have said that substance use, at its core, is a person's search for God. Of course, substances are a false connection to "spirit"—one that can lead to death, not life. The Twelve Steps sprang up as a practical path showing the way to face up to our desires and not be ruled by them. It isn't easy, but it's a challenge with human proportions. It's not something we do once and have it over with. Our lives and our hearts are shaped on a daily basis over time by what we choose to love.

*Today, I am grateful for my freedom to love
the people and the things that give life.*

*Never look down to test the ground before taking
the next step; only he who keeps his eyes fixed on
the far horizon will find his right road.*
— *Dag Hammarskjöld*

When we first learned to drive, we had to develop the
skill of fixing our eyes far down the highway rather than
immediately in front of the car. In our lives, we also need
the bigger picture. When we were caught in our pursuit
of immediate gratification and crisis management, we
didn't have time to look at where it was all leading.

Now we have a better idea of what our bigger goals
are. Larger values guide our choices; we no longer focus
only on immediate relief or satisfying today's appetites.
Naming our goals and our deepest values gives us the
guidance to steer our course smoothly and become the
kind of man we want to be.

*Today, I will name goals and values,
and they will guide me.*

*Not until we are lost do we begin
to understand ourselves.*
— *Henry David Thoreau*

Growth and development never happen in a straight line. Events may surprise and challenge us. A man thinks he is on a path to success and suddenly loses his job. A student takes a challenging class and fails an important test. A professional truck driver is involved in a serious accident. These events that fall into our lives are horrible things to deal with. Yet we have to respond to them. They show us the edge of what we know and force us to push further.

It is always the lost feeling that opens us up to grow and learn. When we are lost, it is in finding ourselves again that we grow deeper.

*Today, I accept the challenges I face because
I have no other option, and I will use them to
shape my growth in a positive direction.*

*Chains do not hold a marriage together. It is
threads, hundreds of tiny threads, which sew
people together through the years.*
— Simone Signoret

A relationship may begin with love at first sight. Some
of us have experienced that feeling many times. But the
growth of a relationship is nurtured by sharing many
experiences and times together. We live through many
kinds of events, including the unexpected turns that
every life brings. We have enjoyable times together, and
we inevitably disappoint each other or frustrate each
other. The history we build over time is the storehouse
of our lives.

Sometimes when a relationship is strained, we easily
say to ourselves, "I could do better without this; I could
find someone else and have a better life." But to walk
away from a relationship would be to walk away from
a shared history. Some relationships are so toxic that it
is better to cut our losses and leave. But usually we are
happier when we can repair the wrongs and build on
our history.

*Today, I am grateful for the history
I share with my intimate partner.*

OCTOBER

I can't stand it when a player whines to me
or his teammates or his wife or the writers
or anyone else. A whiner is almost always
wrong. A winner never whines.

— Paul Brown

Sometimes when we get lost in our complaints about our lot in life, it is just a way of staying stuck. We spin out woeful thoughts about why our life is so difficult. This is just another way of being self-centered. When we are lost in that jungle, we may need someone else to alert us to what we are doing.

Everyone has difficult circumstances. No one gets to choose all the circumstances he faces. Many challenges in life are of our own making, but many others are just random events. The way out of self-pity is to remember that we are just like everyone else. And we, like the whole human race, have the job of making our way through the wilderness of our life. Exactly what we accomplish is less important than what kind of man we are as we do it.

Today, I accept my life and continue to
move ahead and grow as a person.

Not everything that can be counted counts, and
not everything that counts can be counted.
—*Albert Einstein*

In following the healing way, we open ourselves to truths
that can never be established as concrete facts. Some of
us have always been comfortable with a spiritual outlook.
But some of us were hurt by damaging or even abusive
experiences in religious institutions and gave up on them
as meaningless. Now we all come together on a path
that takes a very wide view of spirituality while making
spiritual ideas central.

It is reassuring to learn that one of the greatest sci-
entists of all time had a firm respect for realities that
could not be pointed to or quantified. He excelled in the
practical, objective world of science, and he also knew
about spiritual truth. Now we, too, are learning how our
spiritual life creates miracles we could not bring about
by the force of our will.

Today, I am grateful to be tuned in to those forces
that are outside objective, concrete reality.

Be grateful for luck. Pay the thunder no mind—
listen to the birds. And don't hate nobody.
— Eubie Blake

Some mornings we wake and the bright sun warms our bodies and our spirits. Other mornings we wake to darkness and feel a heavy shroud of worry surrounding us. In order to be present for life, a man needs to carry the big picture of life's cycles in his mind. Small children don't have the big picture. They haven't yet experienced the ups and downs of daily life. But our adult life has taught us that the bad times pass and the bright sun returns.

A strong man doesn't deny the darkness, but he learns to cope with it by choosing what he pays attention to. There may be thunder, but we listen for the birdsong. We don't lose our gratitude for the good luck we have had so far and for the constant companionship of our Higher Power. We care for our relationships, and they sustain us through the darkest times.

Today, I accept the cycles of life, and I am grateful for the good fortune that has carried me this far.

*The more we allow ourselves to be servants of
having, the more we shall let ourselves fall prey
to the gnawing anxiety which having involves.*
— Gabriel Marcel

In our consumer-driven world, we are flooded with
tempting advertising images that promise us happiness,
power, and virility if we buy these products. Success in
this consumer world means financial wealth rather than
good character or playing the hand we are dealt. The
phrase "quality of life" often refers to material wealth,
not to the quality of one's personal relationships.

We are following an alternative path. On this path,
material goods are just trappings to be used and shared,
never to define us. Our worth as a man is never measured
by the car we drive or the clothes we wear. The guy who
drives an old beater and the guy in a hot sports car are
equals. No matter how many toys we have, and no matter
how badly we have screwed up our lives, God loves all
creation and wants the best for us.

*Today, I will keep my eye on the
real ingredients of my "quality of life."*

Despite all the obvious distinctions between men and women, our hearts share the same fears and yearnings. Learning how to hold each other's hearts tenderly is the art of love making.
— David C. Treadway

Intimacy is showing our inner self to another person. When we live in an intimate partnership, our task is to learn to be worthy of the trust and vulnerability our partner opens to us. At the same time, we need to learn to show our fears and yearnings to our beloved. When we make disrespectful, sarcastic, or hurtful comments, we show ourselves as unworthy of the intimate vulnerability our partner granted to us. When we are open and intimate with our partner, we deserve to be treated with tenderness and respect.

This kind of intimacy is not easy to achieve or maintain. It is a very grown-up kind of relationship that we learn to achieve as adults.

Today, I will be vulnerable with my partner and honor my partner's trust in me.

The other planets may not be able to support
life, but it isn't easy on this one either.

—*Anonymous*

The difficulties and pleasures of life always seem to come as a mixture of both. Today's hard problems will be different by tomorrow. And the pleasures and rewards that come our way always come in waves of greater and lesser measure. That perspective on life's problems is what we need to continue on our path of personal growth. Today, we no longer reach for the instant relief of a drug or a behavior to get an immediate good feeling.

In the midst of all the trees, we look up and see the bigger picture of the forest. The problems at hand today will pass. Our task is to examine the problem, then decide what we can do about it and what we can simply turn over to our Higher Power. By keeping our perspective on the bigger picture, we will not get lost in the anxiety of the present moment.

Today, I am grateful that I can count on
my Higher Power for help in dealing
with my difficulties.

Never does the human soul appear so strong and noble as when it forgoes revenge and dares to forgive an injury.
— E. H. Chapin

Forgiveness is a spiritual process. Little children always justify their hitting and aggressive behavior by claiming, "He started it!" Throughout life, we all have justifications for our resentments. We all feel hurt by others at times. Our spiritual journey asks us to face these affronts with a more grown-up mind than we had as small boys. Our immature and undisciplined ego may play a role in how we respond to an offense today.

Much of the time, when we are hurt, another's actions are not really about us. They are a reflection on the person who did them, not on us. We are not in the center of that picture, and if we take our overgrown ego out of it, we can see that. Sometimes we have to defend ourselves, but we don't have to hold on to the resentments. Only after we have grown strong enough can we see that our most dignified response is to let the incident be about the other person, and finally forgive that person.

Today, I will take my ego out of the picture, let others' actions reflect on them, and strive to forgive them.

*Forgiveness ought to be like a canceled note,
torn in two and burned up, so that it can never
be shown against the man.*
— Henry Ward Beecher

When we have been hurt or offended, we naturally have strong feelings about it. Sometimes we want to leap to forgiveness as a cover for our wounds because we fear the damage to the relationship. In that case, forgiveness comes too soon, before we even let ourselves know what we feel. More often, our ego has been bruised and, primitively, it wants revenge. But it is we who carry those angry feelings and nurse our negative inner world. And it is we who must find a way to live in a more positive state of mind.

Some of our angers and resentments may be decades old. No repayment can ever settle the account. Maybe we didn't get what we needed from our parents, or a former spouse treated us badly, or a co-worker or boss was unnecessarily harsh. We can lighten our burden by simply tearing up the unpaid debt. In a spiritual sense, we can leave the other guy's conscience to him and his maker. By declaring old debts forgiven, we are free to live in the present as happier, better men.

*Today, I will strive to let go of old resentments
so I can live more fully in the present.*

*You don't have to suffer to be a poet; adolescence
is enough suffering for anyone.*

— John Ciardi

We can think of our life as a poem. We are crafting a meaningful whole out of chaotic experiences. How do we make something worthwhile from what our life has been? We begin by getting honest with ourselves and others. We all have had enough suffering to feel deeply. We all have come face to face with the stone wall of facts we cannot change by our own efforts.

The ultimate creation of a man's life is in who he becomes. We have lost a lot. We have had sufficient pain, and we are guilty of doing bad things. Now we take that bundle of experiences and ask, "What can I learn from them?" All that we have done can be turned into something heroic and wonderful. There is nothing more inspiring than a mess of a man who works hard and turns himself into a good person.

*Today, I will continue my path to creating
a life with meaning and quality.*

*In America, sex is an obsession; in other parts
of the world it is a fact.*

— Marlene Dietrich

Most of us were given conflicting lessons about sex, and
we were often confused about how to fulfill our sexual
nature. As young boys, some of us were told that our
sexual impulses were bad. At the same time, we were
told that sex is a sacred gift from God. Many of us grew
up to have regrets about our sexual activities. Some of us
were captured by pornography, turning others into sex
objects. And sex became a drug of escape for many of us.

Our spiritual goal is to fulfill our sexual and erotic
nature in joyful, safe, and respectful ways. We move past
our sexual anxieties by accepting the fact that sexual
pleasure is God-given. It is simply a fact of life and its
value depends on how it is used. It is neither the path to
life fulfillment nor the devil's creation. When we align
our sexuality with the rest of our lives, it is a pathway to
connection and intimacy.

*Today, I am grateful for my sexual nature
and will express it in ways that I respect.*

*Love consists in this, that two solitudes protect
and touch and greet each other.*
— *Rainer Maria Rilke*

Mature love is a powerful and wonderful thing that has to be learned in adulthood. Children are certainly capable of loving and receiving love, but they are not yet fully formed as individuals. Adult intimacy is like a bridge spanning the space between two people. When our intimate partner confides in us and becomes vulnerable, our task is to make that moment safe. And when we become vulnerable, we have a right to the same safety— which means no disrespect and no demeaning or abusive behavior. When someone puts trust in us, it is our duty to honor it.

Some of us grew up in families where love was paired with abuse and disrespect. The very people who loved us sometimes deliberately hurt us. As adults, we may find ourselves being more decent and polite to strangers than to our loved ones. This becomes our adult challenge: to act respectfully to our loved ones and protect and honor the trust they have placed in us.

*Today, I will be most respectful of my intimate
partner, who is the most vulnerable to me.*

*Unknowingly we plow the dust of stars, blown
about us by the wind, and drink the universe
in a glass of rain.*

— *Ihab Hassan*

Do we find it difficult to make conscious contact with a
Power greater than ourselves? Does the spiritual plane
seem out of reach? All we need to do is open our consciousness to the awesome big picture. We make contact
with the ages of the universe by simply drinking a glass
of water. The apple we eat is made of atoms and mole-
cules that have been transformed countless times and
only at this moment take the shape of an apple. Next,
they will become part of our human body. This simple
mindfulness puts us in direct contact with the vastness of
space and time. Our senses taste, smell, and feel the contact while our rational mind simply feels awe. We were
brought into being by forces that we cannot explain, and
we will be carried forward on the wave of life. We can
accept this ultimate force and relax into it.

*Today, I will be mindful of my constant contact
with powers I cannot understand.*

Two things a man should never be angry at:
what he can help, and what he cannot help.
— *Thomas Fuller*

In the Serenity Prayer, we pray for the wisdom to know the difference between what we can change and what we cannot. That distinction can be hard for many of us to recognize. When we finally see the reality clearly—that some things we face cannot be controlled by our own will or fixed by force—new possibilities open up to us. When we stop trying to move a mountain, our relationship to the mountain changes. We start to live at peace with the mountain. At the same time, we can take greater responsibility for those parts of our lives that we can change.

Peace of mind comes from accepting what we can do nothing about and taking responsibility for what we can.

Today, I pray for the wisdom that
helps me know the difference.

*If allowed, time and nature will heal you.
Remember that you do not have to heal
yourself. Nature is ready to do it if you step
out of her way and do not present her with
those unnecessary obstacles, despair, and
disappointment.*

—*Dr. Claire Weekes*

The Second Step tells us that a Power greater than ourselves can restore us to sanity. This is the hope Step. It tells us that we don't have to do it; in fact, we cannot do it ourselves. We only have to allow ourselves to receive the help that is flowing toward us right now.

Despair was a common feeling while we were caught up in our codependency and addiction. We knew no other path than to rely on ourselves, and we were defeated. The recovery path gave us a new way to go. Now we need to avoid returning to the old ways or to hopelessness. This new path calls on us to step out of the way, welcome the healing power, and accept the hope that our recovery will proceed.

*Today, I will make the choice to be hopeful
and accept the healing power of nature.*

The older I get, the more convinced I am
that the space between communicating
human beings can be hallowed ground.
— Fred Rogers

When two people sit down and talk, things change. Our true nature is basically revealed in our relationships with others. Starting from infancy, the protection we needed to survive came through our relationships with others. That's how we were formed into human beings. We continue to need that connection in adult forms for our whole lives. To be human is to be in relationship. That's where we learn to know ourselves. That's where we grow and deepen and change. We truly become human by the impact of our communities, our families, our friendships, and our love relationships. If we carefully weigh what we let others know about us, we remain isolated. In that state, we only recycle our single internal conclusions over and over again. But when we let others in and allow them to communicate with some of our best and our worst parts, we step onto a dynamic hallowed ground with rich opportunities for growth.

Today, I will talk to someone about some
of my personal thoughts and feelings.

*The whole life of the individual is nothing but
the process of giving birth to himself; indeed,
we should be fully born when we die.*

— Erich Fromm

We think of childhood as the period of development
and growth. For some reason we regard adulthood as
the time when we should settle down and live as fully
formed individuals. This is not true. Psychologists now
know that in a healthy person, adult development continues throughout life. When we look back five years,
we can see ways that we have changed. Life continues
to present us with new puzzles and new opportunities
to become better men.

We can also be stopped in our development if we
refuse to open up to new growth. An addiction or a codependent way of relating to others can freeze our growth.
When we open ourselves to the truth, we can resolve our
puzzles and seize the opportunities to grow into wiser,
stronger, more generous, honest, and openhearted men.

*I will engage with the reality that today brings,
and I will continue to grow.*

I see God in every human being.
— *Mother Teresa of Calcutta*

In our spiritual development, we learn to see expressions of the creator, the ultimate good, in many places in our daily life. We may imagine that God is a distant figure that we cannot know. But many great spiritual thinkers of various religions teach us to see God within every person. That includes ourselves. We are created by God, and we have a right to be here. No matter what we have done, our being is still a creation of the ultimate, and we ought to hold ourselves in high esteem. When we accept this spiritual truth, what follows is that we honor ourselves and our actions express self-respect.

After we accept that God is within every fiber of our being, we can also greet all fellow human beings with honor for the God within them. This is not something that comes easily or by simple decision. It is a wisdom that grows when we come to terms with our defects and accept them as part of our whole being. We don't have to be perfect to honor the God within us.

Today, I accept the ultimate truth of God
within me and all people I see.

> *Man's powers point to God, but they*
> *cannot understand Him.*
> — *Reinhold Niebuhr*

Our best strengths and greatest powers are signs of God. We have been in trouble because we overestimated our power to control more than we could. Now, on this spiritual path, we have turned to "God *as we understood Him.*" This phrase may make us think we have to define what this Higher Power is in our lives. It can be helpful to think about, but we also do well to accept the limits of our words and our definitions.

Some guys say that they encounter God on a walk through the forest. Some have that experience in a church or temple. Some find God in every living creature. Most great spiritual traditions speak of God as being present everywhere and promise that we are never alone. The powerlessness we learn on this spiritual path includes the human impossibility to contain God in our understanding. To encounter God, we encounter a sense of awe that God exceeds all limits.

> *Today, I am moved and filled*
> *with awe by the spirit of God.*

Do, or do not. There is no "try."
— *Yoda*

Trying is what we do when we aren't willing to make a commitment. We say, "I'll try," when our heart isn't ready to give a full effort. It's what we say when we can't admit that our resolve is wimpy. And it's the lie that will defeat us.

Some challenges we face can't be conquered simply by saying, "I will do it." But we can choose to do something that will help. We can't move the mountain, but we can pick up some rocks. We can engage with the problem and get to know it better. Every action we take leads somewhere and sets us up for the next action. We even learn from our mistakes and that moves us closer to achieving our goal.

Today, I will not just "try"; I will do
something to move toward my goal.

*Everything becomes a little different
as soon as it is spoken out loud.*
— *Hermann Hesse*

Many of us find out what we really think when we start talking. Putting ideas into words is sometimes hard to do, but when we hear ourselves speak, we realize what we have had on our minds. It's an important way to go deeper into knowing ourselves. Other times, we may have thoughts on our minds, but we first connect with the feelings when we say them to another person.

We are social animals, and talking is a crucial part of our humanity. How often do we hear from our partners that we don't talk to them? Maybe they tell us that we "never" talk about our feelings. They love us and crave the connection that talking brings. As we become more at peace with ourselves, we can learn to express more. It takes practice, and we might need to push ourselves to put things into words, but we get even more out of it than our listeners do.

*Today, I will push myself to talk to my
trusted friends and my partner.*

*All the works of God proceed slowly and in
pain; but then, their roots are the sturdier
and their flowering the lovelier.*
— Karolina Gerhardinger

Life is difficult. No one gets through life without some
struggle and pain. But we men in recovery know that our
problems and struggles were the lessons that shaped us
when we were willing to learn. Naturally, we become
impatient and want to get past the difficulties faster.
We look at our neighbors who appear to have easier
lives—and maybe some of them do right now. But we
have our own path to walk, and we must walk in our own
footsteps, not someone else's.

If we had never confronted problems and pain, we
would have nothing to fall back on for the next part
of our life. Our transformation has already progressed.
Because we keep coming back to this program and follow
its guidance one day at a time, the days quickly turn into
months and the months into years, and our roots grow
stronger.

*I will live today with patience and follow
the guidance that my program gives me
as my transformation continues.*

The greatest of all arts is the art of living together.
— William Lyon Phelps

What is this thing called intimacy? It is letting oneself be seen and known to someone who is paying attention. We all want intimacy, and we often don't really know what it is. We confuse sex with intimacy. Many of us have sought the pleasure and excitement of sexual passion as the fast road to intimacy. Many of us focus on what we are looking for in a partner without looking at what we offer as a partner.

True, rewarding, and deep intimacy comes in letting ourselves be known. Sex itself is never more erotic and passionate than when we are emotionally open and honest. That doesn't mean we have license to be a jerk. We can be open and honest, and genuinely put ourselves in someone else's hands, without dumping our disrespectful or hurtful feelings on the other person. When we seek intimacy, the straight line to get there is to let ourselves be known.

Today, I will let my feelings and my history
be known to the one I seek intimacy with.

Approach love and cooking
with reckless abandon.
— H. Jackson Brown Jr.

Our creator made us as loving and sensuous beings. Some have said that it was our search for God, misguided though it was, that led us into addiction and codependency. Some of us have sought nirvana in a bottle, others by compulsively picking up the pieces of someone else's life, and some of us through sex, gambling, or overeating. The fact that we were misguided in our search doesn't negate the fact that we are sensuous and loving men.

We know that the very avenues to pleasure and joy can become paths to our destruction. Now we are learning to handle our emotions directly rather than by covering them with pleasure seeking. We can live a full life while guiding our search for God and for pleasure in more constructive ways. We can give free rein to our love for others without taking over their lives. We can be grown-up, sensuous, passionate lovers with our partners. We can indulge in the pleasure of great flavors without using food to cover our emotions.

Today, I take great pleasure in my loves
and claim my passion and sensuality.

I loved boxing. I loved every minute of it,
every round in the gym, every skip of the
rope, and every foot on the road. The fights
were the dessert.
— *Carmen Basilio, middleweight champion*

Life is about the path, not just the destination. Yes, we have goals and commitments in mind; they give us direction and motivation. But getting there is our life experience. We have some big goals that guide us; they are not accomplished in a day. We live each day in the stream that carries us forward as we gradually loosen our controlling grip.

This path is about the process of moving forward as much as it is about arriving at our destination. We never use the word *cured* because we never have that much control. We only seek to be on the path and stay there, loving our experiences along the way. Once in a while, we enjoy the "dessert" of an achievement, but sharing our lives with loved ones, enjoying a day of good work, taking time to go fishing or dig in the garden—these are the real stuff of a good life.

Today, on my path, I will take pleasure
in what the day brings.

To become a father is not difficult,
but to be a father is.

—*Anonymous*

Many of us grew up with a gap in our hearts, a longing to know our father better, to have his time, his attention, and his love. Where was he? Why did he not get more involved with us? Was his work really that important? Did he really not think about us? Did he care but just not show it?

Our fathers probably grew up with the same images of masculinity that we are dealing with: that we must keep a wall of toughness around us, that we must not show weakness or softness because someone might think less of us. Now, in our recovery and healing, we see that the unfilled yearning was part of our search that led us into problems with addiction and codependency. We were trying to satisfy our needs and soothe our pains, but without effective means. This healing journey includes making peace with our father or the memories we have of him.

Today, I will accept the pain of missing my father,
and I will stand on his shoulders to become a
stronger, more loving man.

We didn't lose the game; we just ran out of time.
— *Vince Lombardi*

On a day when it seems like more things are going wrong than right, we may need to take a longer view. Today is just one day; this week is just one week on a long path. Certainly, there are ups and downs on our path, and sometimes we just need more time.

We can get lost in the details of the moment, when every way we turn seems to show us more frustration. That is when we can get relief by knowing that with more time, we will make progress—and things will look different. Even when we are trying our best and we still don't see the evidence that our lives are getting better, we are actually laying the foundation of a better life. This program of recovery holds promises for us that will be fulfilled as long as we are willing to do the work.

*Today, I will not be discouraged by the frustrations
I face because I believe the promise that my life
will continue to get better.*

*Those who are waiting are waiting very
actively. . . . The secret of waiting is the
faith that the seed has been planted,
that something has begun. A waiting
person is someone who is present to the
moment, who believes that this moment
is the moment.*

— Henri Nouwen

We know that readiness is one of the important ingredients in change. We may have heard the same thing many times in the past, but one day, when someone says it again, we suddenly hear it with ready ears. At that moment, the familiar words hit their target, and we understand a deep truth for the first time.

In recovery, we don't just sit around passively waiting. We actively examine ourselves and our conscience. We practice honesty. We make amends for our wrongs and seek conscious contact with a Higher Power. All these practices are ways to prepare ourselves to receive the gifts of recovery.

> *Today, as I wait for the grace of God,
> I am actively opening myself to receive it.*

*Men can't always do what a man's gotta do
to feel like a man and still do what a man's
gotta do to be a man.*

— Frank Pittman

In this program, we are living a little bit outside of the mainstream. We are more focused on being the real thing than on appearances. In the popular image, a real man is self-sufficient, strong, invulnerable, able to withstand any challenge and go it alone. Playing that role might make us feel like a man, but we are still left with insecurities because we know that inside we are just putting up a front.

To be a man, we are stronger when we are big enough to accept our weaknesses and make no excuses for them. Of course, we don't have to bare our souls to everyone. But we develop genuine, trusting friendships, and we are honest with ourselves and with trusted friends. We show love to our loved ones. We may have been taught that being vulnerable makes us not masculine. But we are amazed to find that we are more approachable and more interesting when we are genuine.

*Today, I accept my vulnerabilities and my
loving feelings and allow my trusted friends
to know me as I am.*

The tragedy of life is what dies
inside a man while he lives.
— *Albert Schweitzer*

It is possible to be spiritually dead while walking around, living and breathing. Many of us have been there. We lost our way. Our hearts and our self-respect were dissolved by alcohol or other drugs, and we became so involved in controlling others that we completely lost contact with the soul at our core. But even at that low ebb, some small glowing ember of spirit remained.

In recovery, the hot embers have been fanned back to life. We may sense that we still have a long way to go, but even that feeling rises from a live spirit within us. It's never a matter of how well developed our spirituality is, but whether we are in touch with it or not. Once we begin to have a relationship with our soul, with our Higher Power, we are alive at our core.

Today, I am grateful for the
spiritual life I am leading.

*Everything that irritates us about others can
lead us to an understanding of ourselves.*
— Carl Jung

In our worst times, we have been irritable and difficult
to live with. That is common among addicts and codependent people. And when we feel most irritable, we are
least likely to look at ourselves. It is very useful now, in
recovery, when someone irritates us, to ask what inside
ourselves makes us so annoyed. We often find that the
very thing that irritates us about someone else is the very
quality in ourselves that we don't want to face.

When another man's whining bugs us, maybe it is our
own capacity for whining that we reject. When someone's self-absorption gets under our skin, maybe we are
sensitive about our own self-centeredness. Sometimes
we find it easier to complain about a quality in others
than to admit we are like that too.

*Today, I will use my feelings of irritation
to guide me inward and know myself better.*

I've failed over and over and over again
in my life and that is why I succeed.
— Michael Jordan

Nobody chooses defeat. The reason we get out there and try our best is that we want to succeed. Failure is painful, and loss can be discouraging. To have a successful life, we need to learn the techniques that successful people use to deal with failure. They know that every attempt has its risks and that we all experience failure. It is in our failures that we learn the most. Everyone on the recovery path knows the pain of great loss and the guilt of facing up to big mistakes. We also take our failures and turn them into net gain by learning the lessons they contain.

Our strength for the future of our lives comes, in part, from mining the resources to be found in the rubble of failure. We refine those resources by our honesty about them. Our experience with what worked and what didn't work points the way to a stronger, wiser life. When we demand resilience from ourselves, we rebound from failure to step forward toward success with our next venture.

Today, I accept that every failure contains
the seeds for success in the future.

NOVEMBER

There's a lot of credit that can be given to youth and enthusiasm, but with them comes foolishness. Age and craftsmanship is not to be played down. I have got more tricks up my sleeves than an alligator has teeth.

— *George Foreman*

As men in the early stages of recovery, we often have felt that we were walking on rubber legs. We felt very shaky. We were ready to admit that our lives had become unmanageable, but to establish a more stable life seemed like an overwhelming challenge. We needed the support of others in the program, people who were ahead of us on this path. So we turned to our sponsors and to other people in our meetings who had walked these Steps before us.

As men who have longer sobriety, we know that we need to share our stories and help others to maintain our own lifesaving recovery. So we continue to attend our meetings as one part of our maintenance program. We become sponsors and share our tricks of recovery because it benefits us as much as the other guy.

Today, as a newcomer to recovery, or as one with more time in, I know that we all have a lot to give.

It is not the employer who pays wages—he only handles the money. It is the product that pays wages.

— *Henry Ford*

Our work gives us meaning and can be the source of many good feelings. Even when we wish we had a better job, we feel good when we do the job we have well. Sometimes at work we get caught up in resentments or personal feelings that tear down our self-esteem. The best tonic for negative feelings at work is to focus on doing a good job, regardless of all the other issues we have to deal with.

Whether we are building complex technical equipment, cutting meat, or managing a team, the product we turn out is the bottom line. It expresses our character. In the long run, an excellent performance will come back to reward us. Knowing that we gave it our best is a source of inner pride.

Today, I know that self-respect comes from doing my job well.

*Change and growth take place when a person
has risked himself and dares to become involved
with experimenting with his life.*
— Herbert A. Otto

On our path, we take the unique circumstances that life
presents and seek ways to use them positively. Our path
is long, with many turns and bends that lead beyond
what we can see in advance. The most cautious person
might hold back from the unknown and try desperately
to control the future. Risk-taking is an important ingredient in good mental health because it opens possibilities
to us that the safest choices will never give us.

We have taken unwise risks in the past and now we
are tempted, in recovery, to hold tightly to safety. But a
balanced life calls us to take constructive risks. We might
risk asking someone to be our sponsor, even when we
don't know how he will respond. We might risk letting
ourselves fall more deeply in love than we have ever been
before. We might risk telling a friend about a long-held
secret, simply to let him know us better. We might risk
applying for a job that will challenge us. There is room
for us to try something, miss our mark, and still learn
from the experience.

*Today, I will feel the thrill and excitement
of taking a constructive risk.*

*Darkness cannot drive out darkness; only light
can do that. Hate cannot drive out hate; only
love can do that.*

— *Dr. Martin Luther King Jr.*

What darkness do we feel in our lives today? Are we troubled by a relationship? Is guilt about past mistakes clouding our peace of mind? Do we feel threatened by a challenge that looms before us? Perhaps we live with an illness or we feel trapped by our life's circumstances. Darkness is universal. It is one side of the coin of life.

We must not respond to this darkness. The question always is, How will we respond? Many times our established ways of responding to our situation only perpetuate the problem. So we must now seek a way to respond differently. We can do the counterintuitive thing. If we can forgive ourselves, it is easier to forgive others. If we first calm ourselves in the face of challenge instead of letting ourselves panic, we will bring our better self to cope with it. If we respond to anger and hate with genuine loving honesty, we may change the nature of a relationship. Light and love are also universal, and we can choose to walk in the light.

*Today, I will respond with calmness
and a loving frame of mind.*

*The will to win means nothing without
the will to prepare.*
— Juma Ikangaa, long-distance runner

Recovery and healing are not a matter of triumphantly grasping victory in our hands, no matter how much we might want to do that. Rather, our part is the hard work of getting ourselves ready to receive the healing that comes to us. The Twelve Steps are the work of preparing ourselves. We can work at learning what it means to surrender; we can work at taking personal inventory—and these things help prepare us.

The healing comes when we are ready, not as something we bought and paid for, but as a gift in response to being ready.

*Today, I will continue to work to ready
myself to receive the gifts of recovery.*

One father is more than a hundred schoolmasters.

— George Herbert

Many of us feel like outsiders in our own families. Who we are and what roles we are meant to play with our loved ones is sometimes unclear. Some of us grew up with absent fathers and may never have learned how to live as fathers in the close circle of love at home.

How can we move from an outsider position—or even an enemy position—into a full relationship with our children? We can begin by showing our real selves. We take the risk of telling them what we care about, what we love, and how we feel. We say what scares us, what breaks our hearts, and what our past was like. The greatest gift we can give is to open our feelings and let our loved ones know us.

These changes do not happen in a day or even a month. But gradually, with repeated expressions of ourselves, in the process of letting ourselves be known, we become loved for who we are, not only for what we can do.

Today, I will tell someone in my family how I feel.

*Truly, when the need is greatest, then God's help
is always nearest. Should we not willingly offer
our hands and heart where help is still possible?*
— *Karolina Gerhardinger*

In the Twelfth Step of our recovery program, we tell our
stories to others who need to hear that there is hope.
As we live in our circle of recovering people, we can
lose sight of the fact that more people still die of their
addictions than recover. We never forget how dismal
and futile life becomes in the grip of addiction and
codependency, and how desperately we needed a way
out. By the grace of God, help was there for us. Now we
find meaning and spiritual growth by telling our stories
of hope to others.

We still can slip into dark moods and self-pity. That is
when we benefit most from reaching out, not so much
to get help as to pass it on to those who need help.
Sometimes the help we give is by inviting someone to
come with us to a meeting. Other times we can give help
by mentoring a young child, donating food to hungry
people, visiting old people who are lonely, or volunteer-
ing at our community celebration.

*Today, I will look for ways to
reach out to others in need.*

Remember that great love and great
achievements involve great risk.
— H. Jackson Brown Jr.

We are not strangers to risk. Many of us have taken huge risks in our addictions and codependency. Looking back at what we put at risk sometimes makes us cringe. Now, in recovery, we may instinctively pull back from any risk. But any good thing can be taken too far. If we refused to take any risk, we'd never fall in love, we'd never reach out a helping hand to someone in need, we'd never take on a project that might yield big rewards.

Our recovery and our willingness to turn our lives over to the care of our Higher Power is an adventure that leads us in unknown directions. The spiritual path is one with interesting and surprising turns. The decision part of turning it over is only the beginning. The next thing we need to learn is to relax and feel comfortable when we are not grabbing control. It takes time and repeated lapses, but each time we return to our trust in God.

Today, I will move forward, not knowing where this
path leads, trusting that things will turn out okay.

*Other things may change us, but we start
and end with family.*

— Anthony Brandt

In our childhoods, our families formed our self-image and our understanding of what relationships are. We learned to either have trust in the system of intimacy that nurtured us, or to distrust the fibers of those close bonds. For some of us, it is easier to trust relationships that aren't close than to feel trust after they become close. Many of us become more fearful and anxious with someone after we are deeply involved with them because we were formed in childhood to feel wary.

As adults, we are still developing and changing. No one reaches adulthood fully formed. Some of us have been stuck in our childhood state. But we are not limited to what we learned as children if we are willing to be challenged to grow in adult love. We have to give ourselves some slack when we make mistakes; there is always room for repair. And we have to grant the same to our loved ones. When we are willing to be honest about our feelings and willing to hear what our loved ones are telling us, we will continue to become better men.

*Today, I continue my adult development
to become a better man.*

*Patience and passage of time do more
than strength and fury.*
— Jean de la Fontaine

It's part of our masculine style: when we see a problem,
we want to get out our tool kit and fix it. We admire
strength and the ability to remedy any problem. That's
not always bad, but as we get older and wiser we learn
that not everything can be fixed with a hammer.

Masculine strength and aggressiveness don't solve all
problems. A savvy man who has been around the block
a few times learns other approaches to problems. We
learn that patience and timing are incredible forces for
accomplishing great things. As we continue to focus on
our own recovery and transformation, sometimes we
feel impatient for the rewards and the peace of mind
that are promised in this program. The best remedy for
impatience is to turn our attention back to the challenges
and the rewards that this particular day brings. They are
sufficient for us to deal with.

*Today, I will remember that time is my
friend and is working on my side.*

A truth that's told with bad intent
Beats all the lies you can invent.
— *William Blake*

Sometimes the truth is the most brutal thing we can deliver. In our recovery, we work very hard to become honest with ourselves, but we must also learn how to handle the truth with others. We are guided to make amends to all those we have harmed, "except when to do so would injure them or others." We must consider our motivations for expressing the truth and see that sometimes privacy and silence aren't dishonest; they are respectful.

The man who apologized out of the blue to a married couple for his affair with the wife did no one any good by his apology. The man who freely gossips about others may speak the truth, but he only gratifies his selfish urges. We are learning to be clear and unflinching in our honesty with ourselves, and gentle and constructive in our honesty with others.

Today, I will tell the truth in
caring and respectful ways.

*All self-knowledge is purchased
at the cost of guilt.*
— *Paul Tillich*

When we take our searching and fearless moral inventory, we walk directly into our feelings of guilt. We have done wrong and hurt people, and there is no longer any hiding from it. That is why we are called to be fearless in our search. A great reward follows our admission, and that reward is the chance to know ourselves and make peace with ourselves.

When we get honest with ourselves about the effects of our actions, we feel the pain that we avoided by denial. It was somehow easier to hide and escape than to stand up to the truth. When we stand up to the responsibility for our actions and their effects on others and ourselves, we actually stand taller and feel more self-respect. Guilt itself is not a bad thing, but holding on to it and leaving it unrepaired is. We may not have known that we were buying something very precious by facing our guilt.

*Today, I will face my responsibilities for my actions
and receive the benefits of knowing myself better.*

Oh God, help me to believe the truth about
myself—no matter how beautiful it is.
— *Macrina Wiederkehr*

We struggle with low confidence and poor self-images. When we try to get honest with ourselves, we often find it easier to see the negative things about ourselves than the positive. A searching and fearless inventory often means admitting the bad stuff. But an equal or greater challenge is to admit the good stuff. If we are to be truly honest, if we are to know ourselves well, we must admit our strengths and our highest qualities. We must not be blind to the best aspects of ourselves. When we look deep inside, perhaps we find a kind heart toward children. Maybe we have reached out to friends when they needed someone. Some of us have been reliable as good providers, even through our worst trouble. All of us have our own unique good qualities to claim, and our journey calls us to be honest about them.

Today, I can name and accept
some good qualities in myself.

*We know what a person thinks, not when he
tells us what he thinks, but by his actions.*
— *Isaac Bashevis Singer*

Until we gain enough self-awareness, we may mistake
our words for the truth. Many of us have developed
patterns of self-deception to serve our addictions and
codependency. It's as if we believe that if we can make
it sound good, it must be true. And if we are good with
words, we can make almost any choice or any action
sound good, especially to ourselves. We also value the
approval of others so we are tempted to say the "right"
thing even if it doesn't match what is in our hearts.

As we grow stronger, we value honesty with ourselves
more deeply. We have greater self-esteem, and we no
longer betray or deceive ourselves. We learn to discern
the difference between "just words" and the truth spoken
from our hearts. Our words no longer cover our actions
or substitute for them; our words help us better understand our actions. Words can now be used to express and
clarify what we do.

*Today, my words will express and clarify
my actions, not obscure them.*

*Hope begins in the dark, the stubborn hope that
if you just show up and try to do the right thing,
the dawn will come.*

— *Anne Lamott*

Darkness is no stranger to any adult. Some of us know
all too well how dark some nights can seem. Many of us
in our darkest hours have even considered ending our
lives. At those times, we feel totally alone and don't see
any hope remaining. And yet, we keep putting one foot
in front of the other, feeling no hope except the hope that
we will find hope. The small flickering light of stubborn
hope continues to burn.

Even when we cannot see the light, dawn always
comes. It doesn't come when we want it to. It doesn't
arrive when we feel we deserve it. Dawn comes on its
own time. What we are required to do is to keep showing up.

*Today, I will keep putting one foot in front
of the other, knowing that darkness and light
are part of the rhythm of life.*

Slump? I ain't in no slump. . . . I just ain't hitting.
— *Yogi Berra*

Flat times in our lives require a bigger perspective. Sometimes we can't pinpoint what is wrong, except that we don't have our usual spirit. We get up in the morning and life seems drab even while the sun smiles through the window. Other times we know that we have good reason to not be "hitting." Ups and downs are natural parts of life.

In the past, we used alcohol, drugs, and other addictive behaviors to escape the feelings of a slump. We never let ourselves feel sad, lonely, or empty, or even get acquainted with what our feelings were all about. But in a healthy, more grown-up life we make room for slumps. We know they aren't permanent, we can tolerate them, and we will feel better later.

We gain perspective by living through it. While walking along a rough path, keeping one eye on the middle distance helps to steady our balance. We know that we have felt better in the past, and we will feel better again.

Today, I will stay on the path.

Any soldier who has been in combat knows that there comes a time after battle, when the smoke has blown away and the dust has settled, when you must lean over and give your foe a hand. For in that moment of generosity, the war is truly over.
— *Frederick Downs Jr.*

Forgiveness is a healing act for both the giver and receiver. It transforms us from unhappy, angry men holding on to old resentments into men who are freed of the past and ready to live at peace in the present.

Forgiveness doesn't mean forgetting. It means that we simply let go of feeling that someone owes us something for past wrongs. It means we write off the bad debts of previous events. Old foes can sometimes even become friends. The foe may have inspired a secret sense of respect in us: how well he fought! We could even say he was a worthy foe and now he can become our respected friend.

What we couldn't see well at close range may become clearer with the distance of time. Personal growth in recovery calls us to name our old enemies and work toward the forgiveness that rewards us with peace of mind.

Today, I will live in the spirit of forgiveness.

*Willingness to accept responsibility for
one's own life is the source from which
self-respect springs.*

— Joan Didion

We all know the struggle with shame and self-blame. It
is a painful issue and has often been the source of many
other bad choices. When we don't think we are very
important, we may dismiss relationships with others as
meaningless; we disappear from them and cause great
harm in the process. We make self-defeating choices
because we feel that we don't really matter anyway. It's
possible to stay in this state of low self-esteem for years,
feeling mystified about how to gain a better self-image.

The truth is both quite simple and challenging. When
we hold values and live by them, we respect ourselves.
This doesn't require perfection. It requires that when
we make mistakes or fall short of our values, we admit
it. By doing so, we reaffirm our respect for our values
even though, this time, our actions didn't match them.
In this way, we remember that who we are is not the
same as what we do.

Today, I will take responsibility for my actions.

Nothing is more desirable than to be released from an affliction, but nothing is more frightening than to be divested of a crutch.

— James Baldwin

We don't realize how attached we are to something until we lose it. Even our burdens can be the focus of our lives. When we have an addiction, we don't want all the problems it creates: the financial woes, the disrupted relationships, the sick and tired feelings. In our codependency, we have relied on our ability to control situations and pick up the pieces after others messed up. But it's very frightening to give up what was our escape.

Everything changes when we see this fear as a spiritual problem. In our addiction mode, we responded from the impulsive part of our brain. Without rationality, we impulsively reached for comfort and pleasure. Now the spiritual path shows us a new alternative. Our fears about giving up our crutch are fears that we will not be safe and comfortable. With a relationship to the God of our understanding, we can rely on a Higher Power to care for anything we fear.

Today, I will not impulsively react to my anxiety. Instead, I will turn it over to my Higher Power and walk confidently forward.

A life lived in fear is a life half lived.
— *Romani saying*

Facing our fears is part of our spiritual development. First, we must admit them. We were raised to be dishonest about our fear, to betray our own consciousness by saying we were not afraid. When we get honest, we see how many things we have avoided, how often we felt tense and uneasy, all because we were afraid. We worry that there won't be enough to fill our needs, that we will be alone, that we won't survive a difficult time. But something mystical happens when we learn at a deep level to turn what we cannot control over to the care of God.

For most of us, we don't absorb this mystery all at once, then live without fear. It is something we keep returning to. We worry about a new responsibility at work . . . and then we remember to turn it over to God and we feel peaceful again. We worry about a trip we will be taking . . . and then we come back to our spiritual peace. We worry about the health of a loved one . . . and then we turn it over. This spiritual practice is a centerpiece of our healing journey.

Today, I will keep returning to the peace that comes when I turn the future over to the care of God.

The breeze at dawn has secrets to tell you. . . .
You must ask for what you really want. Don't go
back to sleep.

— *Rumi*

We were asleep and now we are awake. The breeze that
woke us may have been sharp and biting, but it was a
gift that brought us back to consciousness. We carry
many wants in our hearts. We needed to wake up to
remember them.

On this particular day, we can remind ourselves of
the things we want most and ask our Higher Power to
keep us on our path to find them. It is good to take an
inventory of our deepest desires. Most of all, we want
the healing and recovery that makes all other things
possible. Many of us want to be good fathers to our children. We want to feel love and be good partners to our
intimate mate. We want to be productive and fulfill our
abilities and talents. We want to be good and strong and
generous men.

Today, I am grateful for my awakening
to this renewed life.

*It is our choices . . . that show what we
truly are, far more than our abilities.*
— J. K. Rowling

Intelligence, talent, skill, achievement, and wealth are wonderful assets. But we all know people with these assets whom we don't admire. The man we most admire is the one who plays a bad hand well. No matter how smart or limited a guy may be, how physically strong or weak, or how high or low his job is, what we admire most in a guy is how he deals with his circumstances. Our task today is to make the choices that we respect most, rather than the choices that only serve our hungry egos. We can cultivate a generous, tolerant, self-respecting character by choosing attitudes and actions to express these traits. We can welcome newcomers, forgive those who have hurt us, include those who are different from us, and be generous to everyone.

When we follow that path, we will have the pleasure of friendship and the rewards of self-fulfillment.

Today, I will choose actions that express my best self.

*The self is not something ready-made,
but something in continuous formation
through choice of action.*

— John Dewey

We're not the men we used to be. The little boy who went off to his first day of school so many years ago exists only as a memory. The guy who pursued his controlling behaviors and sought his pleasures and escapes is not the guy who now follows a path of healing and recovery. We build on who we were and the experiences we had, and we continue our formation into a whole self as long as we live. That is why we continue through daily prayer and meditation to look at ourselves and make the choices that will take us further in the direction of a stronger, more self-respecting man. Some of us were frozen in our development and didn't continue to grow in our wisdom and emotional strength. We were seduced by the allure of childish answers and easy escapes from the challenges in our lives. Our formation as adult men was sidetracked and bogged down, going nowhere. Now we have made new choices that put us back on the track that supports our growth.

*Today, I choose to stay on course
to live the life that restores me.*

What is to give light must endure burning.
                              — Viktor Frankl

We all are born into a life that inevitably includes some amount of challenge, pain, and distress mixed with the joy and learning. Our strength and our wisdom grow by dealing with trouble. The wisest people we know—the ones we admire most—have life stories that brought them through dark days of despair and striking difficulties. Their trial by fire sharpened their clarity about what really counts in life and raised their motivation to live by their values.

Life has become better for us in recovery. But no one ever becomes immune to life's problems. We get stronger and wiser in dealing with them. We get better at maintaining our balance when everything seems to push us off balance. As we grow more skilled in dealing with life, our light shines on the path for others seeking their way.

Today, I accept that difficulty is part of life,
and I will learn what it has to teach me.

Gratitude is heaven itself.
— *William Blake*

The feeling of gratefulness sometimes sweeps over us and fills us with a warm glow. We know what it feels like to be lost and frightened, with no compass to point our way out. The great contrast between where we once were and where we are today inspires us to feel thankful. Now we have our lives back. We feel like real men again. We have the companionship of fine people. We have hope for the future.

This feeling of gratitude is an antidote to our struggles with desire. Our desires have taken us places that harmed us. We wanted more control, we wanted more pleasure, we wanted our feelings to stop, and we wanted more than was good for us. We have enough right now. This fullness of gratitude is a wonderful relief from our driving desires.

*Today, my desires are set aside by my gratitude
and the knowledge that I have enough.*

*Experience is what you get when
you don't get what you want.*
— Dan Stanford

We want what we want and we often feel entitled to it, but it's only when reality gives us something else that we get pushed into further growth. We may have a road map to our destination, but if we have car trouble on the way, we will have some unexpected experiences. Our first response to a change in plans is usually frustration or disappointment. We never would have chosen to face the situation. But facing it changes us, and we become a different person. Often the change is small, but some events change us in big ways forever. That is why we are only partly in control of the course our life will take. After we have changed, we become loyal to the new person we are becoming. We appreciate what we learned. When we choose responses that match our integrity, we come out stronger, wiser, and more experienced.

*Today, I will be open to the
experiences that I didn't plan.*

> *If called by a panther*
> *Don't anther.*
> — *Ogden Nash*

We were brought to this program after following our desires and our passions to self-destructive extremes. Sometimes we still hear the call from that dark side, seducing us back to the ecstatic highs. Relapse is always a danger. We never get over being addicts and codependents. No man eradicates his dark side. It's not a bridge we can burn behind us.

How do we prevent the ever-possible relapse? First, we take "One day at a time," accepting that we cannot fight tomorrow's battles today. We don't fret about how we will stay clean and sober in the future. Second, we stay in touch with other people. We keep talking and don't allow ourselves to fall back into old patterns of isolation. When we hear that seductive call, we talk to others about it. We also ask for help in making contingency plans: What will we do if we're tempted to slip, and if we do slip? And third, we take our mistakes and turn them into something productive by learning from them.

> *Today, once again, I admit that I am a*
> *codependent and/or an addict and that my*
> *recovery is a daily process of healing.*

Like all young men, I set out to be a genius,
but mercifully laughter intervened.
— Lawrence Durrell

Self-centeredness is a remnant from our immature past, giving us an inclination to take ourselves too seriously. When we can laugh at our mistakes rather than be ashamed of them, we have come a long way. When we can shed the burden of "specialness," our load is remarkably lighter. When we can let another person's sarcasm reflect back on him rather than allow it into our core, our relationships are simpler and easier. When we can simply participate rather than needing to be the top dog, we have a lot more fun. When we can accept compliments with gratitude and be a humble winner, we like ourselves better.

In our manhood, we strive to achieve, not so that we are better than everyone else, but so that we can fulfill our potential. We want to be the best person we can be, not the best person in our group. We aren't driven to overcome our shame by being perfect. We accept our imperfection as part of universal human nature. Competition can be fun; it doesn't have to put our self-esteem on the line.

Today, I will laugh at myself and
take joy in being human.

*Too many people are thinking of security
instead of opportunity. They seem more
afraid of life than death.*
— *James F. Byrnes*

Life is never fully secure, and those of us who grew up
in stressful households learned early that security was a
precious thing. What we didn't learn was how to reach
out from our security to seek and grasp opportunity. One
problem we may develop in our recovery is overcautious-
ness, which comes out of our frightening memories of
being out of control in our addiction and codependency.

Life is always a risk. Walking up to the plate to take a
swing at the next pitch is a risk, but life is so much richer
for doing so. Part of our recovery is learning to accept
opportunity when it appears and allow for the possibility of mistake. We don't need to condemn ourselves for
having tried; we can learn from every attempt. We are
much more alive for the risks we take and the opportunities we accept.

*Today, my life is richer for the possibilities
that I am moving toward.*

*When you say "yes" to others, make sure
you aren't saying "no" to yourself.*
— Paulo Coelho

In our codependency, we often think first about what others want. We try to make everyone happy and smooth the edges of conflict for everyone else. It seems like such a caring and loving way to live. We may even be so grandiose as to think we can handle frustrations and swallow disappointments better than others can. When we take it to extremes, we are so focused on others that we don't even know our own feelings. Sometimes we act in dishonest ways to protect others, and we get blamed for the failures that inevitably result.

In recovery, we develop the humility to understand that we are no stronger than others, no better able to care for others than they can for themselves. Happiness comes from within each person; we cannot create it in them. Our own peace of mind comes from within us, not from pleasing others. If someone is disappointed in us, we are big enough to accept that. Our first obligation is to take responsibility for ourselves, then we can begin to be generous toward others.

*Today, I will know myself first and accept
that I don't have to please everyone.*

DECEMBER

*Even if you are on the right track, you'll get
run over if you just sit there.*

— Will Rogers

No matter when we started walking this recovery path,
we always need to return to the questions: What Step
am I focusing on today? What lessons do I need to learn
from these events in my life? There is a natural ebb and
flow in the focus of our spiritual lives. Sometimes we
awaken and become highly alert to our life development;
other times we are sleepier about it. We cannot afford to
go to sleep in our spiritual and character development.

It has been asked of people after they relapsed, what
Step were you working just before you relapsed? Usually
the true answer is no Step at all. They have fallen asleep
on the path. There is no cure for addiction or codependency. It is a permanent condition. So we need to keep
walking the Steps.

*Today, I will stay on track by
renewing my focus on my growth.*

I can accept failure. . . . But I
can't accept not trying.
— Michael Jordan

Sometimes failure can be a trap that, if we let it, stops us in our development. We get discouraged and absorb failure as if it defined us. We may indulge in self-pity and wrap ourselves in the "loser" label. It's a painful identity, but there's a payoff: we rationalize that there's no point in risking again, so we won't need to put forth any more effort. That kind of choice is like a hiding place for our true self. We cannot afford to indulge in such hiding places.

On this path, hiding and self-pity only freeze our growth. We must learn to deal with failure as a part of life. We are human and that means we are incomplete as long as we live. We must accept that we will fail at many things on the way to finding achievement. If we block failure, we block success. So our true identity is that of learner, seeker, and adventurer—a man who rebounds from failure and comes back with his best shot.

Today, I will fulfill my true self
and learn from whatever happens.

*Sometimes it is more important to discover
what one cannot do than what one can do.*
— *Lin Yutang*

We've all had to discover for ourselves the truth about
what we cannot do. Until we had uncovered this knowledge, we couldn't take the first Step. We were doomed
to stay locked in a cycle that led nowhere but down. No
matter how much we tried to improve our self-esteem,
no matter how many awards or salary raises we got, we
were going nowhere with our personal life. We first
needed to learn that we could not control some things.

Once we read the unhappy news that we could not
control our addictive behaviors, and we could not control others, we were ready to take the first Step. Then a
whole world opened up to us. Only then were we ready
to learn what we could do. Even now we use that experience as a model for our lives. When we accept what
we cannot control, our understanding of the problem
changes, we become calmer, and new possibilities come
into view.

*Today, I am prepared to learn from
discovering what I cannot control.*

No one can make you feel inferior
without your consent.
— *Eleanor Roosevelt*

When we are oversensitive, when we take offense at a negative comment someone makes to us, we put our self-esteem under that person's control. Whatever a person says is, first of all, a reflection on the speaker. If someone says you look like a pig, that doesn't make it so. Children don't have the inner resources or the emotional independence to hold a separate identity apart from what others say, and they can be crushed by it. Adolescents take great personal offense if someone looks at them wrong. As adults, we have the ability to control our sense of self, even if we haven't yet learned how to use it.

If our partner speaks in a tone that sounds judgmental, our knee-jerk response is to take it into our core. If a co-worker hurls an insult, we might feel injured. If a friend is thoughtless about our feelings, we might take offense. But we can remember that these actions are first of all a reflection on the speaker. We can adopt a detached attitude about others' comments and give them the freedom to say what they like. We are in charge of our self-esteem.

My honesty about my own self-worth stands
on its own. No one else controls that.

Our minds go racing about like horses running wild in the fields, while our emotions remain unmanageable, like monkeys swinging in the trees.

— Dōgen Zenji

When we follow the guidance to pray and meditate every day, we see how busy our minds and emotions are. Often we react out of our emotions, not even knowing we are doing so and believing we are totally rational. The wildness of our inner world is universal and human. Our development as men means taming those horses and monkeys, making friends with them, and training them to work for us rather than running off in all directions.

We grow by getting to know our feelings and thoughts. Emotions are no longer a mystery to us. We can talk about them and express them to trusted friends. After we have come to know what we feel and think, we are less at their mercy and less likely to react on impulse. We know what we are dealing with, and we can choose how we will respond.

Today, I am getting to know those wild horses and monkeys in my mind.

· DECEMBER 6 ·

*Character is what you know you are,
not what others think you are.*
— *Marva Collins and Civia Tamarkin*

True self-esteem is built by having values and living by
them. Many men seek to repair their self-esteem by
going after the praise of others. Praise is nice to get, but
the most highly successful men can still live with an
insatiable hunger, an empty hole in their own self-regard.
Our self-esteem is built by first asking ourselves what our
values are. What do we admire most in a man? What do
we believe is most important in the character of a good
person? What is our highest calling as we live our lives?
When we have the answers to these kinds of questions,
we have a road map to achieving an inner feeling that we
are worthwhile. We don't have to be perfect in fulfilling
those values, but if we use them as our guides, we will
have self-esteem, regardless of whether others praise us.

*Today, I will choose my actions
in accord with my highest values.*

All action ends in passion because the response to our action is out of our hands. That is the mystery of work, the mystery of love, the mystery of friendship, the mystery of community—they always involve waiting.

— Henri Nouwen

In our desire for control, we want not only to say the right thing but to control how it is heard. We want to take an action and have others respond just as we planned. But the spiritual path takes us into the mystery where we accept the truth of what we do not control. We would do well to think of ourselves as an archer. To shoot an arrow, we have to let it go.

We can do our best to say what we sincerely believe and then let others listen and respond. We can do what we believe is the right action and then wait for others to take it where they choose. That is the only authentic dialogue. Our faith comes into play when we engage in the dialogue, knowing that we can only say and do our half of the exchange. Out of the process something real will emerge.

Today, I will live in the mystery of my life, let go of the responses to my actions, and simply wait.

*The day you were born a ladder was set up
to help you escape this world.*

— *Rumi*

In a spiritual life, as our soul develops, our consciousness reaches beyond the mundane world of things, events, and facts. We find meaning in the happenings of our lives: a chance meeting with a friend, a rainstorm that changes our plans, or even our simple daily chores. And we find our connection to the larger whole through friendships and community. We care, we love, and our actions fulfill our sense of who we want to be as men.

Many of us have outgrown or turned away from the religious training we received as boys. Others of us grew within the religions of our childhoods, developing adult spiritual lives. In either case, spiritual development is the process of discovering or uncovering what was there for us, perhaps what was meant for us, from the day we were born.

Today, I am in touch with my soul.

*It has been my philosophy of life that
difficulties vanish when faced boldly.*
— Isaac Asimov

When a serious problem comes into our life, the first
question most of us ask is, Why me?

It's a question with no answer. But we know that being
born means we will face problems and challenges. No
life is free of them. Our development is as much about
learning to deal with problems as it is about learning to
avoid them. Most of us have tried mightily to *not* deal
with our problems by hiding from them or denying them.
We have also tried bulldozing our way over problems
with the force of our will.

Now we have a new tool for facing problems; it's the
paradox of powerlessness. Now we understand that we
cannot control many of life's challenges. When we boldly
face difficulties that we cannot control, we accept the
facts. Accepting our powerlessness over a problem surprisingly makes us stronger. It changes everything. It
even transforms our life.

*Today, I will face difficulty head-on
and admit the situation as I see it.*

What comes from the heart goes to the heart.
— Samuel Taylor Coleridge

Most of what we say and do is laden with implication and feeling. We can say the same words with many different inflections and convey very different meanings. When we have something very important to say, we may worry whether we will be understood. We can rely on the truth that when we speak from our heart to a trusted friend, and when we have his attention, our message will strike a chord.

A man was worried about speaking at a meeting. His friend told him, "Say it from the heart, man! Say it from the heart!" Communication at that level is instantly clear. We all have things in our hearts that we may be afraid to say. We can say them if we remind ourselves that a message from the heart will be heard by the heart. As we grow in our strength and recovery, we become more comfortable, and we speak more and more from that level.

Today, I will keep my heart open and
speak to others from that level.

Among some languages spoken by Native Alaskans, a direct English translation for the term sexual intercourse is "laughing together."

— *Anonymous*

Sexuality is a God-given gift intended to bring pleasure and create bonds between two people. Problems surrounding sexuality are common among recovering men, and it is another area where we can grow. Some of us attached great anxiety to sex and used substances to handle our anxiety. In sobriety, we become faced with the anxiety again. Some of us used sex as our drug, an addiction that served more to escape our feelings than to enrich them.

Our sexual desires and feelings provide energy for our intimate partnership. There is no more shame in having a sexual problem than there is in having a communication problem with someone. We can learn that taking sexual pleasure within a loving relationship is hardly separate from giving it. Talking to our intimate partner and a trusted friend can relieve many problems. Just as we can lighten the burden of any other problem, sexual matters are solvable too.

Today, I am grateful for the pleasure
and the gift of sexuality.

> *There are some defeats more*
> *triumphant than victories.*
> — Michel de Montaigne

The spiritual path is filled with paradox. One example is the word *defeat*, which has a bad reputation. In recovery, we learn that brokenness can be the beginning of changes for the better. Sometimes the drive of our ego takes us on a very exciting but destructive ride. Only in defeat do we open our eyes and begin to understand the deeper truth and go in a direction that fits our better self. That is every man's story in recovery. Out of defeat we find a new form of triumph.

This may be a day in which we face particular worries or losses. Our first thoughts are about the pain and difficulty—we don't yet know what we need to learn from them. We only need to stay focused on the kind of man we choose to be. From that will come the wisdom and the wherewithal to create the kind of life we will feel good about.

> *Today, I am grateful for the sustaining power*
> *of this spiritual life and will stay focused*
> *on the kind of man I choose to be.*

> *The real voyage of discovery consists*
> *not in seeking new landscapes but in*
> *having new eyes.*
>
> — *Marcel Proust*

We have awakened with new eyes as men with new lives. We are walking in the same world but seeing it with new clarity. We were asleep in the darkness, pursuing pleasures that ultimately brought only pain and pursuing control over that which could not be controlled. What once was confusing and beyond the grasp of our understanding we now find simple and interesting in the bright sunlight of our new lives. This path of healing is based on honesty with ourselves and acceptance of our powerlessness.

On this path, we feel like real human beings. We may see that we have much work to do, but we have hope for our lives. Healing has become an exciting adventure. We are gaining a sense of self-esteem, our friendships are deeper, and we are more productive at work. When we feel discouraged, we have new choices for handling our feelings.

> *Today, I am grateful to be awake*
> *and to see the world with new eyes.*

Man is the only kind of varmint who sets
his own trap, baits it, and then steps in it.
— *John Steinbeck*

It's a universal truth that we often reap the results of our own bad choices. We are drawn to substances and behaviors that seem so pleasurable at first, but lead us far astray from the kind of man we want to be. Our bad choices may be self-indulgent escapes from the challenges of life. Ultimately, the escape becomes the trap. We are in the company of millions of would-be escapers, but some of us did a bigger job of it than others. Life as a spiritual path means that we learn from our mistakes and we get better at facing our challenges head-on. There is no need to berate ourselves for being human. When we learn from our experience, it isn't a total loss, and we grow deeper.

Today, I am grateful for what I have already learned,
and I will keep an open mind to continue to learn
from my mistakes.

A problem is a chance for you to do your best.
— *Duke Ellington*

The nature of life is that we are consistently faced with problems. We don't directly choose the puzzle that presents itself to us, but we choose how we will respond to it. The puzzles we get and the responses we choose shape the kind of man we become. Some of us are tempted to balk at our circumstances and refuse to deal with them. We get stuck on the idea that it isn't fair for us to have our particular problem, and we want to quit trying.

Sometimes, facing the fact that we cannot change a problem and accepting it is the highest form of character. Other times, digging deep within ourselves to pull up the best we can muster and facing a difficult challenge turns us into a better man than we thought we could be. The challenge itself is the inspiration that brings out our best.

Today, I will accept the problems I face
and give them the best I can muster.

You must do the thing you
think you cannot do.
— *Eleanor Roosevelt*

We are faced with what we cannot do. We are up against a stone wall. A fundamental wisdom about adulthood is that we have not grown up until we grasp our powerlessness and accept its lessons. Easy answers from the immature and inexperienced tell us to buck up, never give in, and do it alone. Every adult faces this wall in his life, whether he is an addict or codependent or not. If he hasn't faced it or doesn't accept it, he has not yet truly grown into manhood.

When we have tried every tactic and every control maneuver to manage what we cannot change, there is another option. We can accept that we are powerless to change the stone wall. This acceptance feels like defeat at first. But it also makes us wiser and leads to deeper insight about life. In the Twelve Step program, surrender is only the first Step to a new beginning. We are next led to a spiritual connection that makes the impossible possible. Out of the collapse of our old ways can rise a new way of life—and a new man.

Today, I am grateful that I was guided
out of despair into new possibilities.

Until you are willing to let go of your parents,
you continue to conceive of yourself as a child.
— Frederick Perls

Emancipation is a lot more than living away from our parents and supporting ourselves. Many things can still hold us within the limitations of childhood. Some of us haven't shaken the criticisms we heard as children. Some of us still turn to indulgent parents who pick up the pieces and don't expect us to stand on our own two feet. Some of us hold on to resentments about our parents. These things imprison us within our expired childhood.

By its nature, emancipation cannot be handed to us. It is only won by taking it—by our own maturity. Letting go of our parents means we choose to be grown-up and independent. We tear up the IOU and go forward into manhood. After letting our parents go, we can have adult relationships with them and enjoy them for who they are.

Today, I am letting go of my parents so that
I can live in the present as an adult man.

If you are patient in one moment of anger,
you will escape a hundred days of sorrow.
— *Chinese saying*

Anger is a life force. It gives us energy and motivation. Like so many other things, it is not inherently good or evil. The key for us, as developing men, is how we use our anger.

We can all recall times when we felt the power of anger but handled our feelings badly. We popped off impulsively and were filled with regret. Or maybe we couldn't admit our mistake and went to extremes to justify our bad behavior. Some of us have been so frightened by our own anger or someone else's that now we avoid it at all costs.

As adult men, we develop good ways to manage this power. We start by getting acquainted with anger so that we know it when it shows up. We aren't ruled by it, and we aren't afraid to feel anger. This Chinese saying doesn't say to hide from anger. It says to begin with patience. Then we can form an effective way to handle anger so that we won't have regrets.

Today, I will accept my feelings of anger
when they arise, and I will express them
in constructive ways.

Everybody kind of perceives me as being
angry. It's not anger, it's motivation.
— *Roger Clemens*

Anger is not a threat to our recovery, but our failure to channel it and use it well is. Some things deserve anger and should be our targets. Injustice and disrespect to our fellow human beings is a prime example. Out-of-control anger, however, does not serve anyone well.

We can achieve greater peace of mind when we learn to manage our anger rather than hide it. When we learn to focus our anger at worthy targets and express it clearly and directly, without stooping to abusive language or threats, we become much more effective men. That way, anger can be a constructive source of energy, and we can hope to resolve it and make things better. We are learning to take our own inventories and to be honest with ourselves about all of our feelings.

Today, I will examine myself for my angry feelings
and make wise choices about how to manage them.

Be what you is, cuz if you be what you ain't,
then you ain't what you is.
— *Tombstone inscription, Tombstone, Arizona*

Once, a young man felt he needed advice on how to approach someone in whom he was interested; he decided to talk to his grandfather about it. The advice his grandfather gave him was, "Just be yourself." That was easier said than done, but it was good advice. In order to be ourselves, we must first get to know ourselves and then make peace with who we are.

In taking an inventory of ourselves, in admitting our faults and our strengths, and in facing those we have harmed and repairing our mistakes, we are discovering ourselves and accepting ourselves. That is how we fill out our true manhood. No one stands taller than the man who knows himself, with all his weaknesses and all his assets, and accepts himself as he is.

Today, I accept myself and continue
to grow into a better person.

God brought light out of darkness,
*   not out of lesser light;*
God can bring thy summer out of winter,
*   though thou have no spring. . . .*
All occasions invite God's mercies,
*   and all times are God's seasons.*
                                        — *John Donne*

Despair has been no stranger to many of us. We recall times when all spirit and all hope seemed to evaporate. We may still be subject to dark moods. In our bleakest moments, we wonder where to turn for hope. We may see no reason for optimism as we look at our situation. In those difficult times, we are most in need of the support of God, our Higher Power. The greatest spiritual teachers and all the world's great religions tell us that God is present to those most in need.

In our darkest hours, God is with us, within us, beside us, supporting us. Perhaps we experience the presence of God in a call to a friend, a bird lighting on a branch, or a beautiful song on the radio. And out of darkness comes light. Today's difficulties are only one moment in the flow of our lives, and they will change.

Today is another occasion that invites God's mercies.

Courage is not the absence of despair; it is, rather, the capacity to move ahead in spite of despair.
— Rollo May

Some days we wake up to an overwhelming feeling that things look bleak. We see loss and danger around us, and we fear for the future. That is when our character is most tested. That is when we are called to continue to just put one foot in front of the other. There is no need to solve all our problems right away or to change the world immediately. Courage isn't necessarily a feeling of confidence that we can triumph over all odds. It's knowing that we can move ahead one step at a time, and it's taking positive action in the face of our fears. Each day we can do small things that are constructive. By these small things, we can place ourselves on the positive side of life's equation. We can put our weight where we want to go. That is courage.

Today, in the face of my despair, I will focus my efforts on the side of my hopes and values.

Hear me, four quarters of the world—a relative I
am! Give me the strength to walk the soft earth, a
relative to all that is! Give me the eyes to see and
the strength to understand, that I may be like you.
With your power only can I face the winds.
— Black Elk

All of nature upholds us. It is inevitable that we face
strong winds in our lives. These winds challenge us with
losses, sadness, difficulties at our work, frightening dangers, and desires for things that only hurt us. Our spiritual program teaches us that we are not alone. Nature
surrounds us. Perhaps we have never considered that the
bird sitting on the branch is our relative. It breathes air
and has warm blood flowing through its veins just as we
do. Even the tall tree we walk past each day is part of our
family of life. These beings comfort us and can teach us
about how to live. Does the fox in the field worry about
what he will eat next week? No, he only hunts for what
he needs today.

I will open myself to the whole family of life,
to the lessons I can learn, and to the
strength that it can give me.

We make a living by what we get, but we
make a life by what we give.
— *Winston Churchill*

As we grow spiritually, we naturally become more generous. It's a quality of a well-developed person. Rather than being anxious over whether we will have enough— and rather than hungrily seeking more and more—we become more openhearted. We feel more abundant within ourselves and find that our spirit of generosity even adds to our own abundant feelings. Where we see a need, we help out.

A generous person doesn't need to shower others with material gifts. The most precious gifts are things such as paying attention to others, respecting them for who they are, and giving our time. Often a material gift is a symbol of the good feelings in a relationship. In our generosity, we also learn to receive others' gifts to us with humility and respect.

Today, I take pleasure in my spirit of generosity.

*The miracle is this—the more
we share, the more we have.*
— *Leonard Nimoy*

Look around you at the happiest people you know. They
are also the most generous and giving people. A generous
spirit creates its own environment. In recovery, we talk
a lot about gratitude—and we have a lot to be grateful
for. This feeling of gratitude inspires us to be generous
toward others in many different ways. Most sharing is
not of material things but a sharing of our spirit, our
forgiveness, and our respect for others. We can cultivate
a generous spirit by reminding ourselves that we have
enough. We have enough to live well, we are surrounded
by love, we have been forgiven for many wrongs that we
committed, and life is filled with interesting adventure.
When we share from this sense of abundance, our feeling
of well-being only grows.

*Today, I will be generous and sharing toward
the other people I come into contact with.*

The day the child realizes that all adults are imperfect he becomes an adolescent; the day he forgives them he becomes an adult; the day he forgives himself he becomes wise.

— *Alden Nowlan*

Facing up to our wrongs is a foundation stone in our recovery. We have been contending with imperfection since the day we were born, both in ourselves and in others. Forgiveness is central to this whole process. When we admit that we have made a mistake, we affirm our belief in our values at the same time. Nothing is more honorable than saying that we hold a value and admitting that we fell short of it. That guilt is the pathway back to repair and forgiveness.

Shame is a dead-end emotion in which forgiveness doesn't seem possible. In our recovery, we are turning shame into guilt, making repair where it is possible and accepting forgiveness or forgiving ourselves. For many men, accepting forgiveness from ourselves or others is the hardest thing to do. It takes true humility to receive forgiveness because we are admitting that we are imperfect like everyone else; to defy the forgiveness that is available to us is arrogant.

Today, I will try to forgive myself for the ways I have violated my own values.

One of the goals of spiritual practice is to make
conscious what was previously unconscious.
— Dan Millman

We find as we proceed with our recovery that commitment to honesty reveals more to ourselves than to anyone else. We begin by taking the advice of our program to be honest with others as well as ourselves. To our surprise, we realize how much we had hidden from even ourselves. It's called denial. We sincerely missed seeing the elephant that was walking around in the living room. We honestly didn't see what we didn't want to see.

Spiritual practice teaches us to yield to the guidance of our Higher Power and to stop controlling. When we yield in that way and when we are willing to see the truth, we feel that we have awakened. We are amazed at what we now see.

Today, I am grateful for my spiritual awakening
and for the truth it allows me to see.

The spiritual life is about becoming
more at home in your own skin.
— *Parker J. Palmer*

We will not feel serene and at peace with the world every day. Some days we feel distressed and restless, and we want something we may not even be able to name. At their most intense, these feelings are like ravenous hunger or dark dread. We may wish we could escape into another reality—or into the "unreality" of codependency or addiction. But now we have the opportunity to use better, more satisfying methods of coping. When we look at these feelings as spiritual needs, we can use spiritual principles to achieve peace of mind. We can make contact with a trusted friend who will listen respectfully to our feelings. We can remember that our Higher Power is always with us, and we can take quiet time for meditation and reflection. We can spend some time where we feel most connected with God—walking outdoors among trees and gardens, listening to music, or going for a good workout. After we respond to distressed feelings in this way, we get relief and grow stronger without the negatives of our old escapes.

Today, I will follow the spiritual principles that
nurture my life and make me feel better.

Apathy is the behavior of a slave.
— *Richard Wagenvoord*

When we were slaves to addiction and codependency, our values were suppressed and our enthusiasm for life was dampened. We were under the influence of our addictive brain. The prospect of life without our substance and without our controlling behavior seemed dull and very scary.

In recovery, we also recover from dullness and apathy. Life gets interesting and full of possibilities. We shed our turned-off attitude. We drop our cynicism and become believers, open to interesting and exciting opportunities. Having faced our slavery and found a path to freedom, the world opens up to us. We know we have a lot of work to do, but we are willing to suspend our doubts. We see that life can be better for us. Apathy has been replaced by hope and a deep sense of gratitude.

Today, I can see a path to follow that makes me hopeful, and I am full of gratitude for my freedom.

Being on the tightrope is living;
everything else is waiting.
— *Karl Wallenda*

In walking a tightrope, a person has to learn to relax while going forward in a situation filled with risk. If he is tense and keeps his body rigid, he will lose his balance and fall. But if he stays relaxed and keeps his muscles loose while remaining very focused, he can continuously respond and readjust his balance while walking. Then he will experience the exhilaration of success. This is a perfect metaphor for life itself, for growing in an intimate relationship and for growing in recovery.

Life itself is a risk. When we hold on too tight, remain too guarded, and anxiously try to control every factor, we become stiff and reactive rather than calm, focused, and responsive. The guidance of this path teaches us to let go of our anxieties and leads us to peace of mind. When we learn to do that, we can deftly walk our path and more effectively maintain our balance in dealing with whatever comes up.

Today, I will calm myself while
walking on my path.

You cannot step twice into the same river,
for other waters are continually flowing on.
— *Heraclitus*

On this last day of the year, time is on our minds. Naturally, we look back at the year just passing. Whether we feel grateful that it is over, or grateful for the gifts it brought, we can always be grateful to be in this healing program on this day. Some of us took our first Steps in recovery this year, and others marked another year among many years. Once on the path, the critical fact is that we are all brothers, equally seeking the same goal: a sober life and peace of mind.

New Year's Eve is a time for celebrations and parties. For some of us, New Year's Eve in the past was a day of complete immersion in our addiction and codependency. There is no point in giving much attention to regrets. Today our celebration has a deeper spiritual meaning. It's a good time to take stock of how far we have come and for gratitude for the benefits of our recovery. We can look at the challenges we faced and what we learned from them. We can look at the gifts that came into our lives.

Today, I thank God for the gifts that
continue to flow and enhance my life.

Index

About Hazelden Publishing

As part of the Hazelden Betty Ford Foundation, Hazelden Publishing offers both cutting-edge educational resources and inspirational books. Our print and digital works help guide individuals in treatment and recovery, and their loved ones. Professionals who work to prevent and treat addiction also turn to Hazelden Publishing for evidence-based curricula, digital content solutions, and videos for use in schools, treatment programs, correctional programs, and electronic health records systems. We also offer training for implementation of our curricula.

Through published and digital works, Hazelden Publishing extends the reach of healing and hope to individuals, families, and communities affected by addiction and related issues.

For more information about Hazelden publications, please call **800-328-9000**
or visit us online at **hazelden.org/bookstore**.

Other Titles That May Interest You

Three Simple Rules
Uncomplicating Life in Recovery
MICHAEL GRAUBART

For those who are just starting out in a Twelve Step program, the prospect of trying to change drinking, using, or other harmful behaviors can seem overwhelming. The good news is there are just three key things we need to focus on. **Trust God. Clean house. Help others.** *Three Simple Rules* offers a new take on this valuable slogan and explains how these rules can help anyone find fulfilling recovery.

Order No. 3655 (softcover); also available as an ebook.

Cornerstones
*Daily Meditations for the Journey
into Manhood and Recovery*
VICTOR LA CERVA, MD

This collection of daily readings—specifically designed for men new to recovery or working to move beyond internal roadblocks that prevent true personal evolution—offers guidance, inspiration, spirituality, affirmation, and new definitions of manhood for building a life free from substance use and addictions.

Order No. 3518 (softcover); also available as an ebook.

For more information about Hazelden publications,
please call **800-328-9000**
or visit us online at **hazelden.org/bookstore**.